Young Readers Edition

THE BIRDS

Roger Tory Peterson

and the Editors of TIME-LIFE BOOKS

TIME-LIFE BOOKS, NEW YORK

ON THE COVER: Rainbow
Lorikeets, near relatives of the
parrots, macaws and budgerigars,
display the brilliant plumage and
hooked beaks typical of their kind.

TIME
LIFE
BOOKS
®

LIFE WORLD LIBRARY

LIFE NATURE LIBRARY

TIME READING PROGRAM

THE LIFE HISTORY OF THE UNITED STATES

LIFE SCIENCE LIBRARY

GREAT AGES OF MAN

TIME-LIFE LIBRARY OF ART

TIME-LIFE LIBRARY OF AMERICA

FOODS OF THE WORLD

THIS FABULOUS CENTURY

LIFE LIBRARY OF PHOTOGRAPHY

© 1967, 1970 Time Inc. All rights reserved.
Published simultaneously in Canada.
Library of Congress catalogue card number 67-26096

Contents

Introduction

The association of men with birds has been long and close. Birds and men alike are active mostly during the day, so they share a familiar world of color and sound. In ancient times, priests of pagan cults believed that in some way bird flight foretold the future. And for centuries men tried to imitate flight itself—some going so far as to build wings that they attached to their bodies. Though we have finally succeeded in mastering flight, the ponderous machines that take us aloft are no match in grace and flexibility for the soaring, diving, darting, climbing actions of a bird on the wing.

Birds have helped men for thousands of years. The warning cries of geese once saved Rome from surprise attack, and even today canaries warn coal miners of the presence of methane gas. Truly, birds touch us in unexpected ways. They are far more to us than game to be shot or chickadees and cardinals to brighten a suburban winter.

No man is more aware of the importance of birds than Roger Tory Peterson. His *Field Guide to the Birds* of America and subsequent field guides on birds of other countries have made him the world's best known bird expert; his system of identification and his paintings of bird life have revolutionized bird watching. Small wonder that the Editors of TIME-LIFE BOOKS were delighted to have him as the author of this fine volume.

DEAN AMADON
Lamont Curator of Birds
Chairman of the Department of Ornithology
The American Museum of Natural History

THE EARLIEST KNOWN BIRD, *Archaeopteryx* (which means "ancient wing" in Greek), flourished 150 million years ago. The drawing above is based on fossils like the one at left, discovered in Bavaria. Several features show that the creature preserved in stone descended from reptiles: its head is like a lizard's, its jaws have teeth, and its wing bones end in sharp claws. The imprint of feathers, however, prove it was a bird.

1

From Archaeopteryx to Sparrow

What kinds of creatures are birds? Of all the higher animals they are the most beautiful, the most admired and, except for fish, the most numerous. Birds can be found almost everywhere—from the North Pole to the edge of Antarctica, in cities, high in mountains, flying through dense jungle foliage or soaring over forest, prairie or endless tracts of ocean.

A Giant That Could Not Fly

Taller than a man, a seven-foot predatory bird over-shadows a human figure drawn to the same scale. *Diatryma*, whose head was as large as the head of a horse, roamed the plains of North America 60 million years ago, when birds were becoming more numerous but many types of reptiles were dying out. Though feathered, *Diatryma* could not fly, and probably caught its food by running down small reptiles and mammals.

About a century ago birds were first called "glorified reptiles," a good description, for it is certain that the first birds were simply reptilelike creatures with feathers. And it is the feather—not flight—that sets birds apart from other animals.

Life has existed on earth for more than two billion years, but birds are not nearly that old. Fossils, the evidences of animals preserved or imprinted in clay or stone, suggest that the first bird lived about 140 million years ago. This was *Archaeopteryx (pages 6 and 7)*. It was so much like a reptile that scientists would have called it one except for the clear imprint of the creature's feathers visible on the fossil.

Though not quite like a modern bird, *Archaeopteryx* was not a true reptile either. It was, in fact, the link between the two kinds of animals. Its head was lizardlike, its jaws had teeth, its slender tail was reptilian —but it had feathers. It was the size of a pheasant and it probably could only barely fly. It is a good guess that *Archaeopteryx* usually moved by running over the ground

and clawing its way up rocks. Its round wings and long, wide tail indicate that it was a gliding bird that launched itself for short distances, much as the present-day flying squirrel does.

Archaeopteryx is called an "ancestral" bird. This means that it was the bird from which all others have descended. In time the first true birds began to develop and multiply. These were the Neornithes, birds such as *Hesperornis*, a toothed diver four or five feet long, and *Ichthyornis*, a small ternlike sea bird. (Both of these are illustrated on pages 10 and 11.)

Scholars have named the tremendously long era of which our time is a part the Age of Mammals. Early in this era—some 63 to 36 million years ago—many birds closely resembling those of today were to be seen; among them were primitive forms of ostriches, pelicans, herons and ducks. Further on in time—about 36 to 13 million years ago —birds even more modern in appearance came into being. If a bird watcher of today could take a pair of binoculars 20 million years back through time, he would see many

familiar-looking birds. A close inspection, however, would reveal none exactly like those of our time. He would also see birds that look totally unfamiliar—creatures that would later disappear, such as *Phororhacos* (*opposite*), a huge and ungainly bird that could not fly.

In evolutionary terms, the time during which many of the birds alive today came into being was relatively recent—13 to two million years ago. This was the period when birds enjoyed their greatest variety. In those days the earth was home to about 11,600 bird species, one third more than the number alive today. However, in the long history of bird life, even these 11,600 species are only a tiny fraction of the total number that have ever lived. One authority has estimated that since *Archaeopteryx* first took off on a shaky glide, about 1,634,000 different species of birds may have existed. Of these only 8,600 remain. All the rest have vanished, unable to adapt to the vast changes that have taken place on earth.

Today's birds fall into 27 separate major groups which ornithologists—scientists who study birds—call orders. Each order contains a number of entities called species. The word "species" refers to all the birds that are like each other; all robins belong in one species, redheaded woodpeckers in another. Ornithologists look beyond a bird's outward appearance when they place it in an order. Instead they rely on more fundamental factors, such as a bird's anatomy,

HESPERORNIS

ICHTHYORNIS

its skeletal structure or the shape and construction of its feet and beak.

As a general rule those species of birds that evolved first are ranked by ornithologists in the more primitive orders—that is, their internal structures more nearly resemble *Archaeopteryx* than the internal structures of birds that evolved later. Birds in the primitive orders—such as the penguin and ostrich—are less able to adapt themselves to changing conditions than are their more advanced cousins. Finches, for example, belong to the order of birds that are among the most adaptable.

Seeking to explain these similarities and differences, scientists often speak of "adaptive radiation." This means the process by which the descendants of a single species develop along a number of different lines in order to survive. Perhaps the most striking example of radiation can be seen on the remote Galápagos Islands, 600 miles off the coast of Ecuador. Here live 13 species of small, black finchlike birds called Geospizinae. From their appearance, it is clear that all of them are related. A good guess would be that they are all descended from a flock of seed-eating finches that were carried from the continent by a windstorm and took shelter on the islands.

In their new home the Geospizinae had more opportunities for feeding and fewer predators. Their descendants began to adapt themselves to a more diversified diet. Some remained seedeaters. Others developed an

Ancient Birds of the New World

The creatures illustrated here once lived in the Americas. *Hesperornis* and *Ichthyornis*, long-vanished sea birds, flourished 100 million years ago around North America's inland sea, which covered the Great Plains; the man-sized *Phororhacos*, related to the giant *Diatryma (page 9)*, emerged some 70 million years later in South America. *Ichthyornis*, about the size of a pigeon and resembling a modern tern *(pages 18 and 19)*, was a skillful flier, but had small, weak legs. *Hesperornis*, about the size of a small seal, could not fly at all, but made up for this by being a strong swimmer.

PHORORHACOS

The Cassowary: A Land-bound Bird with the Strength to Kill

One of the few birds that cannot fly is the Australian cassowary at left, showing off its bony helmet and pink wattles. This large forest dweller, flightless like the emu and kiwi, is found in Australia and New Guinea. A bold fighter, the cassowary can kill a man with the long sharp nail found on one toe of each foot.

appetite for insects. Still others began to eat cactus. As their eating habits changed, so too did their physical forms. Now some of them have thin bills, others thick, still others of intermediate thickness.

Radiation, as illustrated by the Geospizinae, is one method by which birds have reached their present forms in the course of millions of years of evolution. Another is "convergence," the opposite of radiation. In this case birds that are not related, but that have similar feeding or living habits, develop similar physical appearances because they gather the same kinds of food or seek protection against the same enemies. For example, loons and grebes, birds which closely resemble each other, actually come from quite different ancestral stocks.

Evolution, then, is a constantly changing process. Each of today's 8,600 species of birds might be called a twig on the tree of bird evolution. Some twigs will grow into full branches and sprout twigs of their own; others, as has happened so often in the past, will wither and die. Once a species of bird has formed, it represents a completely different

Text continued on page 17

The 27 Orders of Birds

Every bird in the world is classed in one of the 27 major groups, or orders, listed below according to certain features of its body structure. Some birds that seem to look alike, such as the ostrich and rhea, are placed in separate orders because close study of their muscles, feet and skeletons reveals that they came from different ancestors. This same type of study shows that some birds that appear quite different are actually closely related, like the sandpipers and the puffins. In the list below, the birds are arranged in a sequence that indicates their closest relatives. The painting on the next two pages includes a bird from each order.

ORDER	LIVING FAMILIES	LIVING SPECIES
1 SPHENISCIFORMES: Penguins	1	15
2 STRUTHIONIFORMES: ostriches	1	1
3 CASUARIIFORMES: cassowaries, emus	2	4
4 APTERYGIFORMES: kiwis	1	3
5 RHEIFORMES: rheas	1	2
6 TINAMIFORMES: tinamous	1	42
7 GAVIIFORMES: loons	1	4
8 PODICIPEDIFORMES: grebes	1	17
9 PROCELLARIIFORMES: albatrosses, etc.	4	81
10 PELECANIFORMES: pelicans, cormorants, etc.	6	50
11 CICONIIFORMES: herons, flamingos, etc.	6	117
12 ANSERIFORMES: ducks, swans, geese, etc.	2	149
13 FALCONIFORMES: vultures, eagles, etc.	5	274
14 GALLIFORMES: grouse, turkeys, etc.	7	250
15 GRUIFORMES: cranes, rails, coots, etc.	12	185
16 CHARADRIIFORMES: sandpipers, gulls, etc.	16	293
17 COLUMBIFORMES: pigeons, sandgrouse	2	301
18 PSITTACIFORMES: macaws, parrots, etc.	1	317
19 CUCULIFORMES: touracos, cuckoos	2	143
20 STRIGIFORMES: owls	2	132
21 CAPRIMULGIFORMES: nightjars, frogmouths	5	92
22 APODIFORMES: hummingbirds, swifts	3	388
23 COLIIFORMES: mousebirds	1	6
24 TROGONIFORMES: trogons	1	35
25 CORACIIFORMES: rollers, kingfishers, etc.	10	192
26 PICIFORMES: toucans, woodpeckers, etc.	6	377
27 PASSERIFORMES: sparrows, larks, etc.	55	5,110
TOTALS	155	8,580

26 RED-BREASTED TOUCAN

24 QUETZAL

17 PINTAIL GREEN PIGEON

20 SPECTACLED OWL

2 OSTRICH

5 RHEA

12 MANDARIN DUCK

3 AUSTRALIAN CASSOWARY

4 KIWI

14 GOLDEN PHEASANT

1 ROCKHOPPER PENGUIN

6 CRESTED TINAMOU

16 PHEASANT-TAILED JACANA

22 STREAMERTAIL

27 RED BIRD OF PARADISE

23 WHITE-HEADED MOUSEBIRD

18 GOLD AND BLUE MACAW

25 LILAC-BREASTED ROLLER

9 BLACK-BROWED ALBATROSS

19 RED-CRESTED TOURACO

THE
27 ORDERS OF BIRDS
(One Example from Each)

21 PENNANT-WINGED NIGHTJAR

11 GLOSSY IBIS

10 BROWN PELICAN

15 DEMOISELLE CRANE

13 WHITE-HEADED VULTURE

7 ARCTIC LOON

8 GREAT CRESTED GREBE

Roger Tory Peterson

The Largest and Smallest Birds

Extremes in size among the birds are the two shown here. The ostrich, a ponderous, flightless creature, often weighs 300 pounds. The dainty, buzzing hummingbird, by contrast, may weigh less than a penny. Although the ostrich is the largest living bird, larger species were seen by primitive men not many centuries ago. One of these, a moa, lived in New Zealand until it was hunted to extinction in the 14th Century.

twig from all others, and normally there is no mating between species. Yet all species are part of the same bird tree, and therefore they are all related—in a sense, like 10th or 12th cousins among human beings, some as closely as first cousins.

Yet, related as they are, bird species display an overwhelming variety. The smallest, the hummingbird, weighs less than a penny; however, the largest, the eight-foot ostrich, weighs more than 300 pounds. The difference in their sizes can be seen in the picture opposite. Not many centuries ago there lived birds even larger than the ostrich. Among them were the moas of New Zealand, which sometimes grew 12 feet tall and may have weighed 520 pounds. The elephant bird, as its name suggests, was even bigger. Some may have weighed half a ton.

Just as the penguin and albatross are examples of radiation, two other groups, the tinamous and partridges, show the effects of convergence. The tinamou, an inhabitant of Latin America, is a chunky, almost tailless species that lays glossy, colorful eggs. A bird watcher from North America sighting a tinamou might think he has seen a partridge. But the two birds are not even of the same order. Their ways of life, however, are similar, and this fact has caused them, through eons of evolution, to develop into lookalikes.

In the process of radiation the ostrich lost its ability to fly. This large bird developed living habits much like those of a mammal. In the company of zebras or gazelles, the ostrich grazes over the African grasslands. Perhaps to make up for its inability to fly, this fleet-footed giant can run as fast as 35 miles per hour.

The rhea of South America belongs to an order almost as low in rank as the ostrich. The two birds might be mistaken for close relatives except that the rhea lacks the ostrich's handsome plumes. While the cassowary (*page 12*) and the emu of Australia share the ostrich's ungainly appearance, they are at least handsomer than the kiwi of New Zealand, strangest of all birds living today. The kiwi's wings are so small that they are almost not there at all; and because its

Wide-ranging, Sociable Birds

Royal terns, filling the sky around their communal nesting colony on the South Carolina shore, are related to a number of other groups such as the gulls, auks, puffins, sandpipers and plovers. This large order of water birds is found nearly everywhere in the world, even in the Arctic and at the edge of Antarctica.

feathers are extremely thin and coarse, the bird looks like a football that has somehow grown hair.

Far removed from the earth-bound kiwis are the far-flying albatrosses, petrels and shearwaters. These belong to the order of "tube-nosed swimmers," so called because

the nostrils are in short tubes. Birds belonging to this order range from the swallow-sized black-and-white storm petrels to the wandering albatross, whose wings span more than 11 feet.

The word "albatross" comes from the Portuguese *alcatraz*, a type of water bucket. This was the name Portuguese sailors gave to large sea birds, especially the pelicans with their bucketlike lower beaks. Pelicans, however, belong to a closely related order, the "totipalmate swimmers." These birds, which live by fishing, have pouches—small in the cormorants and frigate birds, but enormous

A Gallery of Living Birds

All birds share certain features: feathers, wings and toothless bills. However, the birds portrayed on these pages show how wide a range of species has developed within this framework—from the flashy toucan to the somber owl; from the penguin, which thrives in sub-zero temperature, to the mousebird, which lives at the equator; from the proud pheasant and the colorful trogon to the comical kiwi; from the soaring gannet to the flightless rhea; from the kingfisher, which eats many things, to the limpkin, which eats only snails.

KEEL-BILLED TOUCAN BAR-TAILED TROGON

in the pelican (the pelican's pouch can hold three gallons of water).

Even within the same order there is often a good deal of variety. One of the best examples of how birds have fitted themselves to their surroundings is the order of "long-legged waders." There are about 120 species in this order, including herons, storks and ibises. All have long stiltlike legs for moving in shallow water and long necks for reaching down below the surface. They eat small fish, frogs and other forms of water life, and

their bills are of many shapes—daggerlike, spearlike, upturned, down-turned, shoelike or spoonlike—so that each may hunt for its own food in the way best suited to its surroundings. The flamingo, for example, has a bent bill with fringed lips, a perfect design for straining tiny edible organisms from the souplike mud in which the bird wades.

The physical forms of the birds of prey—hawks, vultures, eagles, condors—also reflect the way they live. All of the 270 species in this order are powerful fliers, capable of ef-

LIMPKIN LINEATED PHEASANT COMMON RHEA

STYGIAN OWL   GAUDICHAUD'S KINGFISHER   WHITE-CHEEKED MOUSEBIRD

fortless soaring and great bursts of speed. They all have hooked beaks, and most of them have strong, sharp talons for grabbing and holding on to their victims. The vulture's feet, however, are weaker, for it feeds on dead bodies—food that cannot escape. Owls, once thought to be in the same order as birds of prey, are actually very different in structure, but because they are hunters, they have developed some features quite similar to those of true birds of prey.

Fowl-like birds—such as the turkey, quail, pheasant and the familiar chicken—also have very strong feet, but there the similarity to the birds of prey ends. A chicken's foot is designed not to subdue and tear at a victim but to scratch and dig for seeds. In fact the fowls—domestic and wild—are prime targets for the birds of prey.

The cranes, rails, coots, bustards and related families, some 185 species in all, belong to an order called "marsh and prairie birds." The stately cranes are storklike, whereas rails and coots are more like hens

COMMON KIWI   GENTOO PENGUIN   CAPE GANNET

Two Closely Related Pigeons with Different Plumage

The ornate head feathers of the Victoria crowned pigeon *(near right)* are part of the elaborate plumage that make it different in appearance from the smaller, plainer white-crowned pigeon *(opposite)*. But more important than outer differences are the similar body structures that make them members of the same order. All pigeons, for example, suck up water rather than tilt their heads back to swallow, as do other birds. This order, called the *Columbiformes*, includes the extinct dodo and the present-day sand grouse.

and hide in the reeds. The bustards are heavy-bodied walking birds that live on the treeless plains. All these species are very ancient. Their survival is in doubt as man continues to reclaim swamp land for farming and other purposes.

It is apparent that the way a bird looks has little to do with its relationship to other birds. Nowhere is this more evident than in the order that includes perching birds. This is the largest of all orders, numbering 5,110 species divided into about 55 families. Members of this order range in size and beauty from the tiny, homely wrens to the large and elegant birds of paradise and lyrebirds.

Naturalists and ornithologists have often attempted to list birds in another way, by relating each species to geography. This has not been wholly satisfactory, for members of a species are sometimes found in widely separated places. A number of European birds, such as the house sparrow and the starling, have found perfectly acceptable homes in the Americas.

Attempts to list birds according to climate are also likely to fail. Some birds, such as the horned lark, seem as comfortable in the Arctic as on the hot Mexican tableland. The common raven, one of the most

widely distributed birds in the northern half of the world, lives in such varied surroundings as the waterless Sahara, the forests of Canada and the seacoast of western North America.

How many birds are there? One estimate places the number of birds in the world at about 100 billion. For the United States, a good guess might be about six billion land birds, or almost three per acre. Just how many sea birds there are is anybody's guess, but the number is in the hundreds of millions.

Many birds, particularly sea birds, live in large colonies. Sometimes the population of one colony numbers hundreds of thousands. Perhaps the largest single mass of sea birds ever sighted was observed off the Australian coast. The flight, made up of shearwaters, which look like small gulls, may have numbered as many as 150 million birds. Penguins also gather in colonies by the hundreds of thousands, while auks of the Arctic and sub-Arctic waters and sooty terns of the Indian Ocean both live in colonies of more than a million.

If we rule out birds that gather in large colonies, it is estimated that in the United States the greatest concentrations of birds are found in plant-rich swamps and southern hardwood forests. These areas sometimes support as many as 15 or 16 birds per acre. At the other extreme are the western prairies and short-grass plains, which can barely support a single bird per acre.

What is North America's No. 1 bird? Some might think that it is the house sparrow. Others favor the familiar starling. The most common American bird is probably either the robin or the red-winged blackbird. Found coast to coast, both are very adaptable. Among the rarest birds on this continent are the Eskimo curlew and the ivory-billed woodpecker. Once numerous, both have now almost disappeared—in other words they are almost extinct.

The whooping crane is another bird threatened with extinction. After being ruthlessly hunted, and many of their breeding grounds drained, they almost vanished. In 1916 it became illegal to shoot them, and under this shield the birds began to make a comeback.

Since 1941 their numbers have more than doubled, but in 1966 there were still only 43 of these birds alive in the wild.

The greatest destroyer of bird life is not the hunter but starvation. When a species' natural feeding ground can no longer support it, the species will disappear unless men take measures to preserve it. On the other hand the population of a species will greatly increase when food becomes more abundant. Recently in a Canadian forest the population of nesting warblers grew to an extraordinary degree during a plague of spruce budworm. The warblers did very well on a diet of these insects and a great many were able to produce large families. But as the number of insects declined, so did the warbler population; excess birds could not nest. This is a stern way, perhaps, to maintain a balance between warbler and insect, but nonetheless it is nature's effective method of checking population explosions within the enormous family of birds.

An Odd Beak That Is Bent to Hold Squirmy Meals

The strange, broad bill of the four-foot-tall shoebill stork is useful for holding slippery frogs as well as for cracking the shells of small turtles. As in the case of the shoebill, birds have evolved a variety of bills that help cope with different types of food. Thus, the pelican's deep pouch for holding fish and the eagle's hooked beak for tearing at flesh are examples of some of the physical adaptations geared to survival.

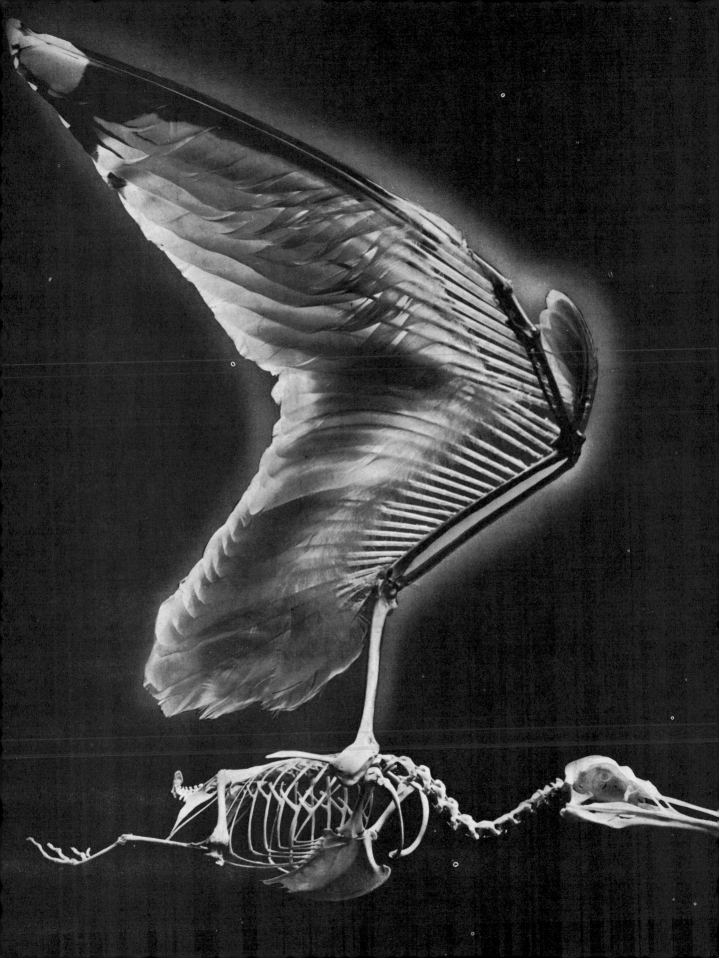

2
A Unique Anatomy for Life on the Wing

THE LIGHT SKELETON and feathers of a gull, like those of most birds, are masterly designs that rival those of modern airplanes. Birds' natural airframes have many features especially suited for flying: hollow bones, a deep breastbone for anchoring wing muscles and a knoblike tail for controlling tail feathers.

Although a few birds cannot fly, the vast majority have physical features specifically designed for life on the wing. After birds branched off from the reptiles they developed in such a way as to make flight not only possible but as easy for them as walking is for men. For weight reduction, even their bones became hollow, resembling dry macaroni.

Since flying demands a rigid airframe, the rib cage and backbone of birds were joined together in a stiff structure. Only the neck and tail—and of course the wings—remained flexible. The breastbone developed into a large, flattened extension called a keel; the keel serves as the anchorage for the enormous flight muscles. These muscles may make up from 15 per cent of the body weight to a remarkable 30 per cent in some hummingbirds, whose tiny but powerful wings become a blur of rapid movement as they hover in one spot or even fly backward.

The body structure that developed in birds over millions of years is both light in weight and remarkably strong; it is better designed for flight than the most advanced airplanes.

The most important single factor in the

27

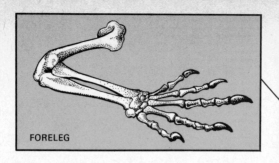

FORELEG

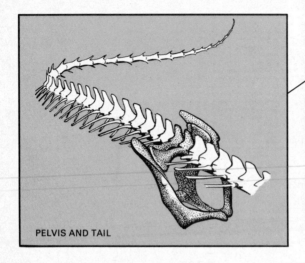

PELVIS AND TAIL

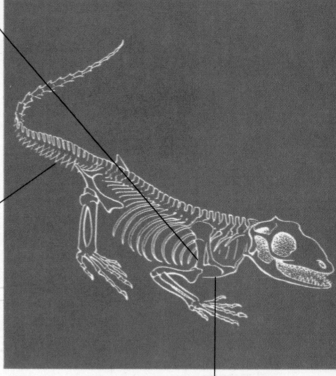

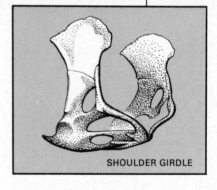

SHOULDER GIRDLE

The Bones of a Reptile

Although both animals are descended from ancient reptiles, the modern lizard differs quite a bit from the bird on the opposite page. The lizard's heavy shoulder structure is strong, but its breastbone is shallow. The short foreleg has a flexible, complex wrist and a five-toed foot for swift running; the body pivots at the waist, or pelvis, using the long tail for balance.

bird's design for flight is the feather. True, there are nonfeathered animals, such as bats and insects, that can fly, but none do it so well as the bird. The feather is a marvel of natural engineering. It is at once extremely light and structurally strong. It is much more versatile than the stretched skin on which a bat supports itself in flight or the rigid structure of an airplane's wing—and far more easily repaired or replaced when damaged.

Look at the drawing of the quill feather of a pigeon (*pages 30 and 31*). The center shaft of the feather provides stiffness where support is needed, yet it is flexible toward its tip. This flexibility permits the bird to change its direction in a fraction of a second. If the feather is placed under a microscope, its complex design leaps into view. The center shaft supports numerous side shafts called barbs. Each barb, in turn, supports even smaller

28

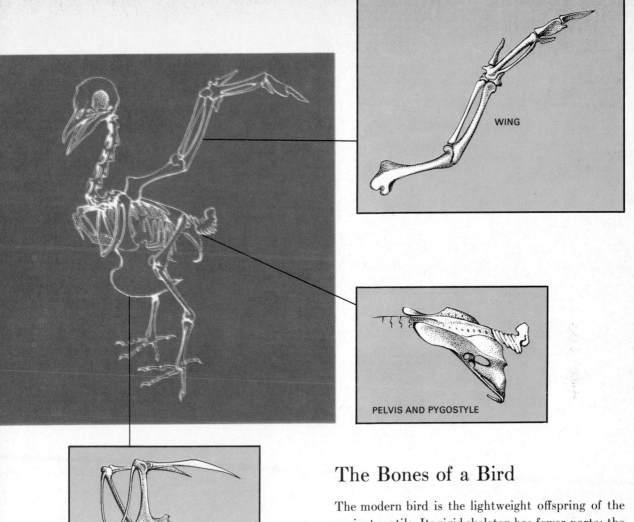

WING

PELVIS AND PYGOSTYLE

SHOULDER GIRDLE

The Bones of a Bird

The modern bird is the lightweight offspring of the ancient reptile. Its rigid skeleton has fewer parts; the two collarbones, for example, are joined into one "wishbone." Its wings are simply forelegs that hold feathers on the arm, wrist and three-fingered hand. Tail feathers are fastened close to a bone called the pygostyle, the leftover remnant of the lizard's tail.

barbs called barbules, which have their own tinier barbs called barbicels. Many barbicels end in microscopic hooks that lock together and hold everything neatly in place. A single pigeon feather may have several hundred thousand barbules and millions of barbicels and hooks.

The webbing of the feather is soft, yet firm; you can easily separate the barbs by running a finger down the feather against the grain, and just as easily bring them together again by running a finger up. The opening and closing action can be compared with that of a zipper.

How did this structural marvel develop? Basically a feather is a scale like those found on snakes and other reptiles. Reptiles have thousands of scales that cover and protect their bodies. It is likely that, when birds began their development from reptiles millions

Feathers: Reptile Scales Gone Fancy through Evolution

The long quill, called a "flight feather," when examined under a microscope (*closeup, left*), shows the structure that has evolved from simple reptile scales. In the course of millions of years of evolution, the scales became stiff shafts out of which grow hundreds of barbs, each one looking like a miniature feather. These barbs have even smaller barbs growing out from them, with hooks that mesh together. During flight, the bird may twist and flatten these feathers.

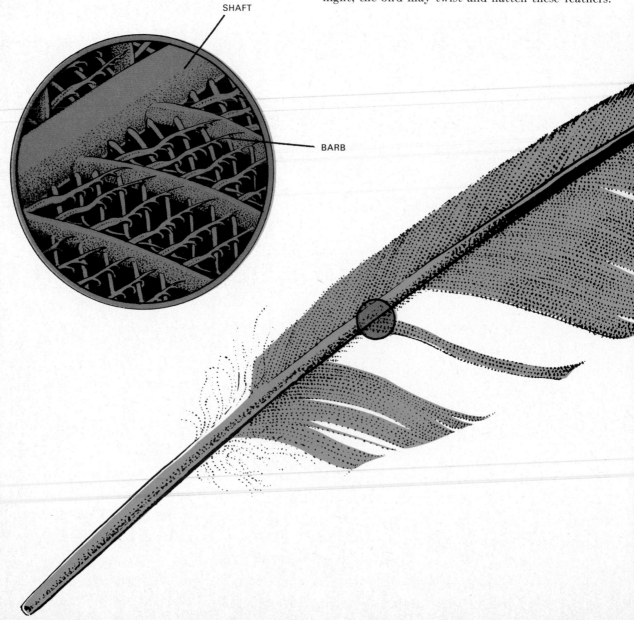

SHAFT

BARB

of years ago, their feathers were little more than long, loosely attached scales. Eventually as the scales grew ever longer, the outer edges frayed and spread until they changed into true feathers. In fact, birds still have reptilian scales on their feet and legs.

The feathers on a bird's body are called contour feathers because they give the creature its outer form. Under the contour feathers are filoplumes—weak, hairlike shafts with short tufts and barbs. These are the "hairs" that a housewife might singe from a plucked chicken. On many birds, there are also down feathers—soft, shaftless tufts, hidden under the contour feathers.

Feathers help birds in other ways besides aiding flight. As an extremely light, tough, durable padding, they protect the bird's thin, sensitive skin and act as an efficient air conditioner, trapping body heat when the weather is cold and allowing body heat to escape when it is warm. They also form crests, beards and other brightly colored embellishments, with which males and females attract each other.

How many feathers does a bird have? There are almost as many answers as there are

Wings That Open and Close to Lift Birds into the Air

A bird's wing, like an airplane's, is streamlined to cut through the air easily, but it has special features because the bird flaps its wings up and down. When the bird lifts its wing on the upstroke *(top)*, some of the feathers spread apart to let air slip through and make the wing easier to raise. On the downstroke *(bottom)* that powers the bird's flight, these feathers hold firm, overlapping each other to press solidly against the air.

different species, but generally the larger the bird, the more numerous its feathers. A patient dairyman once counted all the feathers on a hen: there were 8,325. Another investigator spent days plucking 25,216 feathers from a swan. Songbirds, on the other hand, may have as few as 1,100 feathers—though the count varies not only from species to species but from season to season. Just as human beings shed clothes in hot weather, birds shed feathers.

Feathers, though they are tough, are often broken. Therefore every full grown bird must cast off its old set and grow a completely new cloak—a process called molting —at least once a year, usually in late summer. While the bird is undergoing this process, it may have a few gaps in its rows of flight feathers, but usually these gaps do not seriously affect the bird's ability to fly. The exceptions to this rule are ducks, geese and certain other waterfowl that cannot fly during the molting period. But these birds, which can find their food in the water or on the ground, are less dependent on flight for survival than are most other birds.

The shape of a bird's wing *(opposite)* is yet another example of superb design for flight. It is thick and blunt along the forward edge to part the air more effectively, and bladelike in back to speed the passage of the wing through the air. The underside of the wing is flat or slightly concave—like a shallow, inverted bowl—to increase its lifting power. The upper surface is more rounded to allow the air to flow over it smoothly. Only the straight, "arm" halves of the wings are used for lift, except when the bird is gliding or soaring. The "hand" parts of the wings— the tips—are generally used as "propellers" and "rudders" to enable the bird to move up, down or forward. In this respect the design of a bird's wing differs radically from that of an airplane's—whose propellers (if it has them) are often located on the wings, but are not really part of the wings.

Thousands of articles have been written about how birds fly, but a bird's wing is so complicated, and it has so many flexible mov-

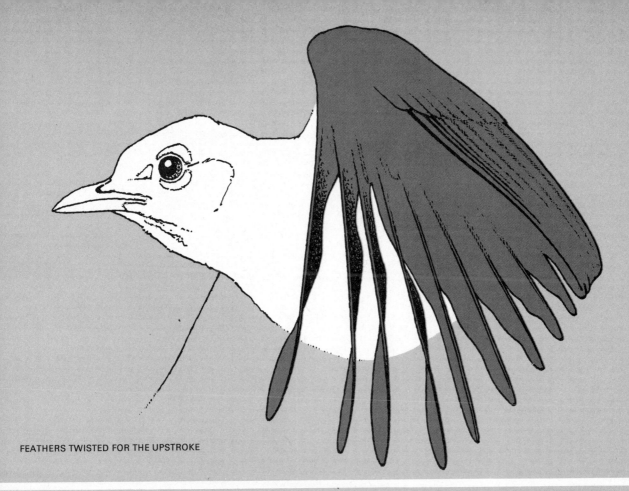

FEATHERS TWISTED FOR THE UPSTROKE

FEATHERS FLATTENED FOR THE DOWNSTROKE

The Twisting Feathers That Propel Birds in Forward Flight

To move ahead, ducks, and other birds, use their feathers in almost the same way that airplanes use propellers. For a bird, the propellers are the strong primary feathers at its wing tips. On the downstroke (*above*) the bird twists these primaries, which bite into the air like a propeller. This pulls the bird forward. On the upstroke (*opposite page*) the inner part of the wing close to the shoulder gives lift to keep the bird aloft.

ing parts that twist and bend under the pressure of the air, that it is almost impossible to give an exact description of how the wing does its job. However, we do have some general information.

During flapping flight (*as shown above*) each of the bird's "propellers" moves in a half circle—forward on the downstroke to pull the bird along, then backward on the upbeat. At the moment when the downstroke ends and the upstroke begins, the flexible feathers of the wing tip part, like the fingers of an outspread hand. This permits air to slip through freely without hindering forward motion. During the upstroke, the "arm" portion of the wing continues to lift the bird so that it can stay at the same height and not dip downward between strokes.

The larger the bird, the slower the wing beat. The huge pelican may flap its wings as slowly as 1.3 times per second, a pigeon

five to eight times, a mockingbird 14. A ruby-throated hummingbird may beat its wings at the fantastic rate of 70 times per second.

As the ornithologist Crawford Greenewalt has pointed out, nature changed the rules in designing the hummingbird. All other birds move their wings freely at three joints that link the wing structure together: the shoulder, where the wing is attached to the keel bone; the elbow, where the wing can be bent outward; and the wrist, where the hand feathers are attached. But in a hummingbird the wing is almost all hand, and the only joint that moves with ease is the shoulder joint, which attaches the wing to the keel bone. It is almost as if the human hand and shoulder were joined directly with no arm between.

One important result of the hummingbird's structure is that the circular action of its wings (*pages 36 and 37*), which is similar to that of insects, gives it a flight that resembles the helicopter's rather than the airplane's. Like the helicopter, it can hover almost motionless over a blossom, it can move backward or forward by tilting its wings and it can rise directly from the ground without a forward run. Slow-motion movies show how the hummingbird flies backward: by a downward scoop of the tail and backward tilt of the wings.

Far less complicated than the hovering flight of the hummingbird or the flapping of most other birds is the simple glide.

Gliding was undoubtedly the way the earliest birds flew; creatures such as *Archaeopteryx* probably climbed up rocks and trees and then launched themselves on rigid wings for short flights. Pelicans glide while traveling in formation. So do geese and other birds when they are coming in for a landing. Gliding saves energy, but gravity and conditions of the air limit the distance a bird can glide before it must flap its wings again.

Much greater skill is needed for soaring. Soaring birds make use of rising air currents as do pilots of motorless gliders. Soaring birds make such effective use of air currents that for long periods they do not flap their wings at all.

The hawks are masters at soaring for long periods while resting their muscles. On sunny days when the thermals—currents of warm air that rise straight up—ascend from the heated earth, bird watchers can observe red-tailed hawks, turkey vultures and sometimes even eagles, as they soar in wide and graceful circles on invisible columns of air.

To most people, the sight of flying birds—whether they are gliding, flapping, hovering or soaring—has an almost magic beauty.

There are few things in this world more thrilling than the sight of a vulture or a condor as it glides on motionless wings along the face of a cliff. Effortlessly the bird soars in and out of canyons that no airplane pilot would dare to enter.

Coming in for a landing, the bird first drops its "retractable landing gear"—its feet. Reducing its wingspread with a shrug of the shoulders, it loses altitude, then plunges straight at the ledge. At precisely the right moment, the bird slows its fall by cupping its wings; in this position, the wings offer resistance to the air, thus decreasing the bird's speed, but at the same time the wings continue to support the bird in the air until it spreads and lowers its tail and lands directly on target. For the briefest moment the bird holds its wings high over its body, then neatly folds them in. The contrast between

the bird's ability to control its landing with such precise delicacy and a jet airliner's need for a long, smooth concrete runway makes man's flying machines seem crude indeed.

The most effortless bird flight of all is that of the large albatrosses. Their realm is the sea, where there are few of the warm rising currents that assist soaring birds on land. However, ocean winds are stronger at a height of 50 feet than they are near the sea's surface. The wandering albatross, with its wing span of 11 feet or more, takes every possible advantage of these winds. First it climbs to the level of the faster wind currents and uses them for its long downwind glide on motionless, deeply curved wings, gaining speed as it descends. When it is almost brushing the wave crests, it streaks along the ocean's surface, searching for food, and lands on the water to eat. Then with the slightest shift of its

The Hovering Hummingbird, Which Stands Still in Mid-Air

Acrobats of the air, hummingbirds can fly straight up and even backward. But their most remarkable feat is hovering motionless while sipping nectar from a flower. The views below show the wing action during the bird's helicopterlike flight. Hummingbirds can do these stunts because their wings, unlike those of most birds, are rigid, with little "wrist" and "elbow" movement. In hovering, the bird moves its wings forward and back, but they are twisted in such a way as to give upward lift but no forward movement.

feathers, it climbs again, its great speed sending it zooming upward. By gliding down and zooming up in this way, the bird can fly over the sea for hours without beating its wings.

The flight of birds is an awesome spectacle. But to the birds themselves flight is a practical necessity to help them find food. In their search, birds are also aided by superb eyesight, much superior to man's, with which they can spot a tiny morsel from high in the sky. They are helped by their beaks as well. Each species of bird has a beak especially designed for its way of life. Chickens, for example, have small, curved bills, excellent for picking up tiny seeds; hawks, on the other hand, have sharp, strong hooked beaks to help them tear apart flesh. When we consider how vital to life the eyes and the bill are to a bird, it is no wonder that the skull (*opposite*), once it has been stripped of feathers and skin, seems to be all beak and eye sockets, for these organs are the bird's most valuable possessions next to its wings.

The Bones of a Bird Built for a Life in the Air

An owl's skull shows the features that, with some variations, are found in all birds: large eye sockets, bones that are paper-thin, joined together and reinforced. Most bird bones are hollow, and some of them even have internal braces to add strength without adding weight. A frigate bird with a seven-foot wingspread may weigh three pounds, but its skeleton may weigh as little as four ounces—less than the bird's feathers.

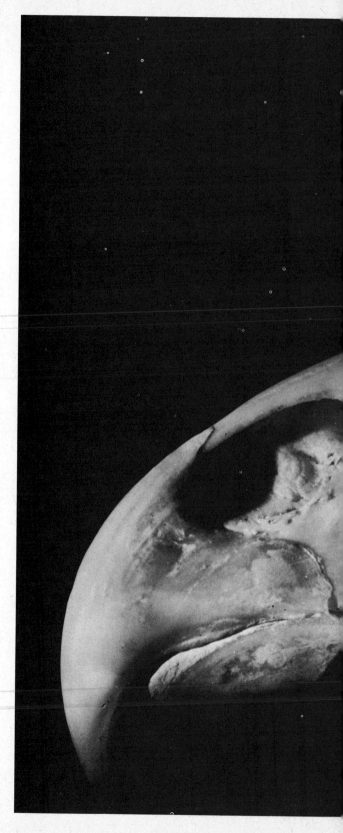

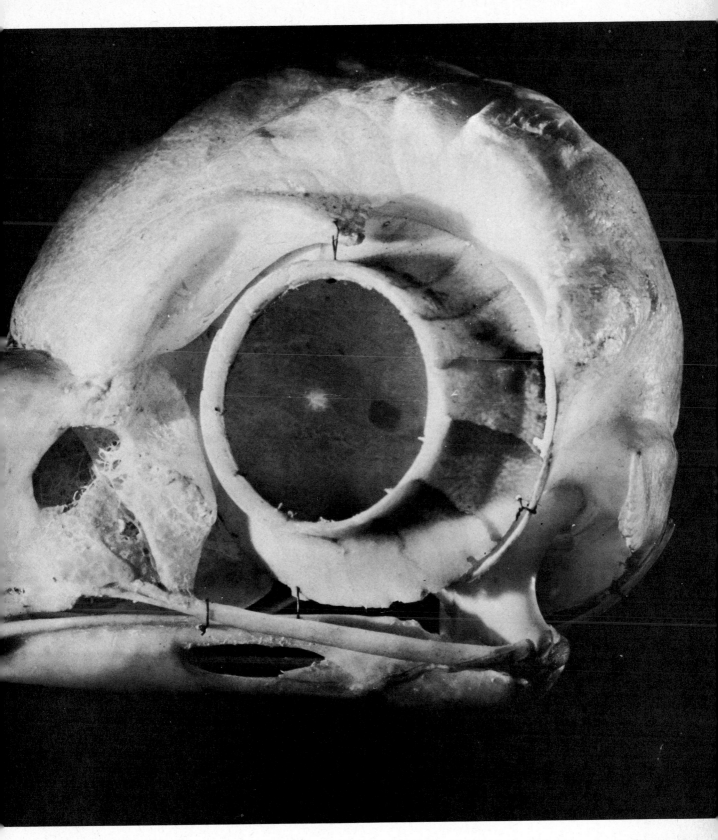

3
The Mystery of Bird Migration

Since man first began watching birds, he has wondered about their disappearance in the fall and their return in the spring. It was a most baffling and intriguing mystery, to which many different solutions have been offered through the ages.

Aristotle, the great philosopher of Classical Greece, believed that though some birds flew south for the winter, others went into hiding. He even went so far as to suggest that certain birds actually changed their physical forms from one season to the next. He believed that the European robin, for example, changed into a redstart as spring turned into summer.

For 2,000 years such ideas were repeated by countless authors. Even more imaginative suggestions were made. Perhaps the most outrageous was the 18th Century belief that birds flew to the moon in winter.

HARMLESS SCARLET DYE, coloring this once-white gull, makes it easier to spot the bird in motion. When painted, birds can be followed until the end of the season, when they shed their colored feathers. Workers in this New England Coast project were aided by the color, in their study of the bird's habits and its range.

41

Strange Colors in the Sky
in an Experiment for Science

A freshly sprayed, bright-hued gull lands among its normally colored fellows. Other gulls apparently see nothing odd in the dyed birds, although they occasionally startle human beings. In 1955, after a spraying experiment by the California Department of Fish and Game, observers all the way up to the Arctic Ocean phoned in tales of pink, green and yellow geese.

Migration usually means to leave home forever to establish a new home in some distant place. But with birds, migration means a round trip, a yearly voyage from summer to winter feeding grounds and back again.

For example, the golden plover and other shore birds in the far-northern regions find plenty of food during the brief arctic summer. But for the other eight or nine months of the year no shore bird could survive in that cold country. However, 8,000 miles to the south, the grasslands of Argentina offer a similar diet—and a warmer climate. As autumn's chill winds come to the northern region, the golden plovers start their long journey to the land far south of the equator, where spring is just beginning. When the season changes once more, the golden plover reverses its direction and returns to the north. In this way the bird enjoys two summers each year and never knows winter's cold and hardships.

Some birds do not migrate. The willow ptarmigan, an arctic grouse that turns white in winter, stays all year in the frozen north. It shifts its diet in winter from insects to the buds and twigs of willows.

The majority of North American and European birds, however, migrate vast distances twice each year (*pages 46 to 49*). In fact, more than one third of all the world's bird species migrate with the seasons.

It is from the northern half of the world that most migratory birds come, escaping each year from winter by flying to their feeding grounds in the south. A large number of European and North American species fly across the equator to spend the winter deep in Africa or South America. Very few land birds of the southern continents reverse the process. When winter comes to their breeding grounds, they may fly toward the equator, but most do not cross it.

Among southern sea birds, however, there are several that do cross the equator to invade northern oceans. Wilson's petrel leaves its nesting grounds at the edge of the Antarctic each year, just as winter is coming to the home area, to hunt for food as far north as the waters off Newfoundland. Greater shearwaters from remote South Atlantic islands range north to Greenland.

On the other side of the world, the slender-billed shearwater, the "mutton bird" of Australia, wanders in a great loop through the Pacific from Bass Strait off southeast Australia, past Japan to the Bering Sea and back again to its home waters, after flying down the west coast of North America. The most amazing thing is that these millions of shearwaters are said to return to the same tiny islands off Australia on the same evening in late November of every year.

Migration is the most dangerous and adventuresome time in the life of a bird. Hundreds of millions of migrating birds never reach their goals. Some people think that birds have a built-in weather-forecasting ability, but this is not true. Though they can sense the changing of the seasons, birds can-

Bands for Tracking the Routes of Wandering Birds

Aluminum bands (*above*), arranged to fit different-sized birds, are the most effective means of tracing bird travels, for they record where and when the bird was banded. More than half the 600,000 North American birds banded each year are songbirds tagged by amateurs; game birds, like the pin-tailed duck (*below*), are usually banded by federal wildlife agents.

ALASKA
324
222

GREENLAND
196
58

YUKON
178
126

NORTHWEST TERRITORIES
266
182

BRITISH
COLUMBIA
384
276

ALBERTA
317
246

MANITOBA
319
245

LABRADOR
162
88

NEWFOUNDLAND
260
128

SASKATCHEWAN
316

ONTARIO
366
267

QUEBEC
328
228

NEW
BRUNSWICK
316
166

PRINCE
EDWARD ISLE
222
103

WASH.
350
235

MONTANA
335
224

N. DAKOTA
307
171

MINN.
358
224

MAINE
350
176

NOVA SCOTIA
313
160

OREGON
360
232

IDAHO
300

WYOMING
343
222

S. DAKOTA
340
207

WISC.
350
203

MICHIGAN
333
202

VT
310
175

N. HAMPSHIRE
340
175

N.Y.
412
220

MASS.
400+
177

NEVADA
322
224

UTAH
325
220

COLORADO
430
235

NEBRASKA
388
194

IOWA
361
154

ILL.
360
160

IND.
321
151

OHIO
340
180

PENNA.
340
185

N.J.
387
181

CONN.
347
158

R.I.
333
141

CALIFORNIA
461
286

KANSAS
380
175

370
175

MISSOURI

KY.
312
153

W. VA.
293
156

365
179

VIRGINIA

DELAWARE
334
160

ARIZONA
433
246

NEW MEX.
400
247

OKLA.
400+
180

ARK.
310
130

TENN.
306
160

N. CAROLINA
357
178

MARYLAND
346
192

MISS.
323
130

ALA
350
145

340
160

S. CAROLINA
368
152

TEXAS
545
300

LA.
395
158

GEORGIA

FLORIDA
405
160

MEXICO
970
750

HAWAII
171 (including 14 extinct)
80

UNITED STATES
including Alaska and Hawaii
840
695

CANADA
520
414

WEST INDIES
493
300

Birds of the New World and Old

The figures on these two maps give the world census of species, by area, as reported by nearly 100 leading ornithologists. Black numbers show how many species are recorded for each region; these include permanent residents as well as occasional visitors. Colored numbers report how many species breed there.

not foresee the storms, winds or fogs that they meet during their journeys. Strong winds sometimes carry them so far to sea at night that they are unable to find their way back to land in the morning. Fog seems to confuse their sense of direction; on misty

ICELAND
231
76

ALL EUROPE
exclusive of U.S.S.R.
577
420

FINLAND
328
203

NORWAY
333
220

SWEDEN
356
240

JAPAN
425
218

INDIA
1,125
920

CHINA
including Tibet
1,100

341
183
DENMARK

IRELAND
338
133

GREAT BRITAIN
(England, Scotland
and Wales)
440
190

364
184
HOLLAND

U.S.S.R.
704
622

BELGIUM
343
148

GERMANY
435
250

POLAND
370
230

300
190
CZECHOSLOVAKIA

338
215

FRANCE
441
260

SWITZ
347
186

AUSTRIA

HUNGARY
332
185

ROMANIA
345
240

PORTUGAL
315
180

SPAIN
397
225

ITALY
450
282

YUGOSLAVIA
236

BULGARIA
338
236

339
204
GREECE

An Endless Country Job

nights lights attract them, so that they often crash head on into lighthouses or high, lighted buildings.

Another man-made problem for migrating birds is the light beams that sweep the night skies over every large airport. Birds

The number of species shown on these maps is approximate, and will certainly grow as more observers join the search. High figures in areas like Great Britain reflect many years of work by armies of watchers. Unfortunately, figures for observed species in Yugoslavia and breeding species in Idaho were not available.

Paths of Long-Distance Fliers

The maps on these pages and the two following show the major routes followed by four far-flying migratory birds. The greatest travelers of all are the arctic terns, who leave their scattered northern colonies in late summer for the 10,000-mile trip to seas near Antarctica. Some pick a route through the Pacific; others go by way of the west coast of Europe and Africa.

Going the Long Way Around

White storks summer in Europe, but spend the winter in South Africa, Arabia and India. Expert gliders who prefer to ride air currents that rise on land, they will fly over water only if they can see land beyond. Thus some have a problem crossing the Mediterranean. Most of the storks bypass the sea by going through Asia Minor; others make a short crossing at Gibraltar.

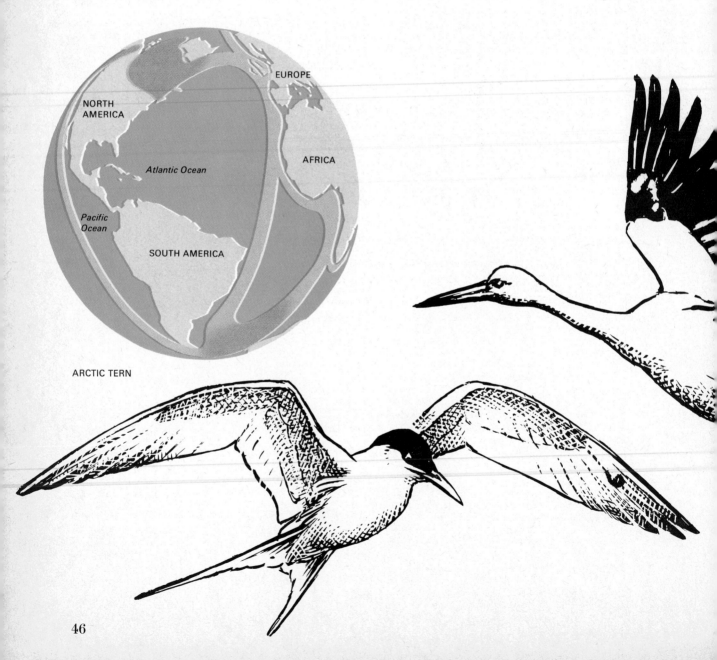

EUROPE

NORTH AMERICA

AFRICA

Atlantic Ocean

Pacific Ocean

SOUTH AMERICA

ARCTIC TERN

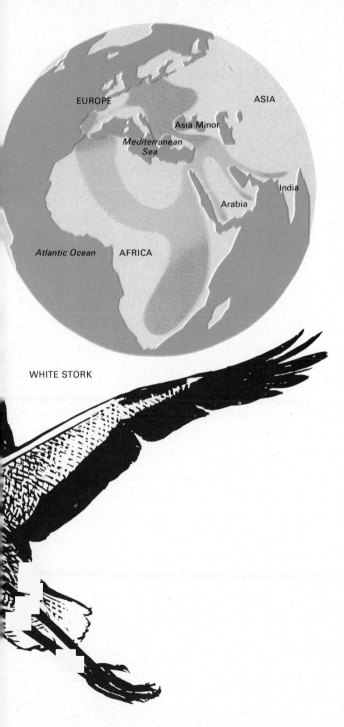

EUROPE
ASIA
Asia Minor
Mediterranean
Sea
India
Arabia
Atlantic Ocean
AFRICA

WHITE STORK

are often confused by such beams and plunge to the ground. At Robins Air Force Base in Georgia, 50,000 birds were killed in a single night, diverted by such a beam.

Natural hazards, however, are far more dangerous. On the nights of March 13 and 14, 1904, millions of Lapland longspurs were caught in a snowstorm in Minnesota and Iowa. Confused, and with feathers heavy and soggy with snow, they crashed into buildings, wires and poles. The next morning the bodies of 750,000 longspurs were found on the ice of two ponds.

Hurricanes can carry sea birds as much as 2,000 miles from their home seas, to drop exhausted on unfamiliar shores. Since the peak of the hurricane season comes at the same time as the fall migrations of many small birds to the West Indies, a single storm can mean death to millions of them. A ship entering the windless eye of a tropical storm has found the air full of small land birds that sought rest and shelter on the decks and rigging.

But if millions of birds die each year during their migrations, the fact remains that billions survive wind, rain, fog and man-made obstacles to complete their journeys—and this is one of nature's great wonders.

To collect some basic facts about migration, amateur and professional naturalists in recent times have tagged millions of birds with lightweight leg bands for identification (page 43) and sprayed others (page 40) so that their flights could be mapped and their

A Long Detour toward the East to Traditional Routes

A land bird that breeds in North American clover fields, the bobolink migrates to the grassy pampas of Argentina by island-hopping through the Caribbean. Members of the small bobolink colonies in the Northwestern U.S. shun the most direct route to the south through Mexico; instead they make a detour east to fly with their brothers along their traditional paths.

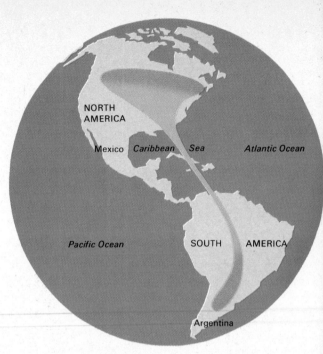

destinations recorded. The first birdbander in the United States was John James Audubon, the pioneer of bird studies in America. In the early 1800s he tied silver threads to the legs of two young phoebes, one of which returned the following year.

Today banding is carried on all over the world. In the United States and Canada alone, more than 2,000 banders mark about 600,000 birds every year. Over the years more than 20 million birds have been banded, and about one and a half million bands have been recovered by bird watchers.

Catching birds for banding sometimes is a problem, and banders employ spectacular methods for capturing them. Whole flocks of geese, for example, have been captured with great nets that are shot up and over resting birds. Wary hawks are tricked by decoy pigeons; when the hawk strikes, a

mechanism entangles it in a net. Small birds are caught in fine, almost invisible nets.

Some of the journeys that banding has permitted men to follow and record are almost unbelievable. An arctic tern (page 46), banded on the coast of Labrador, was picked up 90 days later on the coast of southeast Africa, 9,000 miles away. Another of this species was banded on the Arctic coast of Russia and recaptured near Australia, more than 19,000 miles from its starting point. There is no question that the arctic tern is the champion long-distance migratory bird, but many other birds also fly thousands of miles each year.

Although naturalists often speak of the "routes" or "flyways" followed by birds in their migrations, there is probably not a single square mile of the earth's surface, except for the polar icecaps over which birds

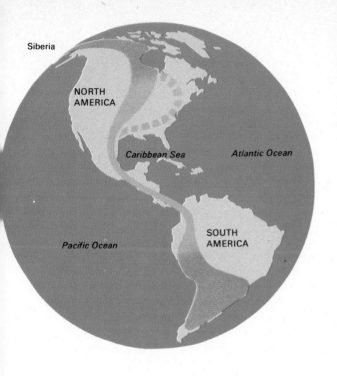

Seasonal Passages from the Arctic Ocean to South America

From its breeding ground on arctic shores, the pectoral sandpiper flies south to winter in South America, always keeping land in sight. The main route crosses the Great Plains, though some birds fly first toward the Atlantic (*broken line*). This species has spread into Siberia, but the Asian birds still cross over into America before making their autumn trip to the south.

do not fly. Yet migrating birds do follow general patterns of flight.

Small land birds, which do most of their long-distance flying at night, generally fly with the airflow—northward in the spring on warm air masses coming up from the south, southward in the fall on cool winds flowing down from the north. These air currents move in broad waves and the nighttime migrators spread themselves more or less evenly throughout the mass of moving air.

Land birds that migrate by day tend to use their eyes to guide them, recognizing such checkpoints as river valleys, coastlines and ridges. Although there seem to be principal routes, day-migrating land birds may switch from one route to another during the course of their journeys.

Daytime migrators have a greater tendency to fly in large groups than do night fliers.

Some well-organized flocks of ducks, geese and swans are packed in such great formations that they almost fill the sky as they fly on their migratory journeys. Swallows travel by day in small, loose companies and gather in larger flocks at their nighttime resting places. In the United States and Canada, grackles, starlings and red-winged blackbirds are mainly day migrants, as are robins, waxwings, goldfinches and many other species.

The first birds to return north are mostly day migrants. The robin, often called a harbinger of spring, may vary its arrival by as much as two to three weeks from year to year, depending on the time when reasonably warm weather returns to the north.

How does a bird know when to begin its migration? We know that birds undergo internal physical changes just before and just after the nesting season. It is during these periods of change that most birds migrate. And we know too, that one of the forces that seems to start these changes is light—the lengthening day of spring, the shortening day of autumn. When the right day arrives, a bird does not have to think about it; its whole body tells it that the time has come.

Birds must be very strong indeed to travel immense distances, and no creatures on earth are hardier. Long-distance migrants store large supplies of food in the form of body fat before beginning their journeys, just as camels store water in their body tissues before undertaking a desert crossing.

But the greatest wonder of migration is the ability of birds to fly thousands of miles without getting lost.

Birds rarely fly in a straight line to their goals; shifting winds sometimes carry them far off course, and even when wind is not a factor, they may not follow a direct route to their destinations. Birds that cross great stretches of ocean do not even have landmarks as guides. Yet somehow, unless they are destroyed by a natural or man-made obstacle, the birds usually find their goals.

Studies have shown that some day-flying birds may use the position of the sun, in addition to landmarks, to help them navigate. Some internal sense enables them to use the sun as a compass that points out directions and keeps them generally on course. When the angle of the sun changes, the bird, in some mysterious way, takes account of the change and is able to adjust its course.

Similarly, experiments with night migrants show that they seem to navigate by the stars. Much like sailors, birds may know that a particular star points the way.

But the exact manner in which birds may use the sun and the stars as a "road map" to their migratory goals remains a mystery. Every time men think they have found the answers, something happens to make them doubt it. Perhaps some day a bright young biologist will unravel the answer to one of man's oldest questions. But even then, the wonder of bird migration will remain, for it is truly one of nature's greatest miracles.

Remarkable Flight Formations That Proclaim the Autumn

On their journey to warmer grounds, ducks cross the sky in the V-formations often seen in the autumn. At the point of the V, the leader breaks trail through the air, and each following bird gets a lift from currents rising off the wing of the bird ahead. Experiments have shown that some birds may use the sun and the stars to find their way on these migrations.

4

The Vocabulary of Bird "Talk"

A MALE RUFFED GROUSE beats his wings to make a drumming sound, which is a proclamation to other male grouse nearby that he has staked out a territory as his own. This drumming is one kind of bird song, the "language" with which birds talk to each other. While most birds "speak" in musical sounds, woodpeckers tap and woodcock flap their wings and tails.

Birds, like people, are social creatures. There are exceptions, of course; certain of them, including grouse, kingfishers, herons (when they are not nesting) and some birds of prey, live solitary lives. But most birds seem to enjoy one another's company.

Doing things together requires a language —a means by which birds can "talk" among themselves. Birds communicate not only with their voices but also with their bodies. The different ways in which they spread their feathers, dart about in the sky, prance about the ground and open their bills all seem to have special meanings for other birds of the same species.

Men have long tried to understand what birds are saying; in Biblical times, King Solomon, reputedly the wisest of men, was supposed to possess the secret of how to talk with birds. While scientists today are learning more and more about the habits of birds, they would never make such a claim. Yet in a general way ornithologists have learned to understand many of the sounds and gestures made by birds.

Why do birds sing and what do their songs mean? First we must decide what a bird song

A Built-in Instinct to Beg

From the moment it breaks out of its shell, the baby herring gull starts begging by pecking at a bright red spot on its parent's bill, receiving in return a bit of fish. By making a test, experts proved that it is the presence of this color that sets off the pecking: when the dummy heads shown here were offered to nestlings, they pecked at all except the one that did not have a spot (*top*). They even pecked at the red pencil with the contrasting white rings at its tip (*bottom*).

is. It takes more than one "cheep" or "peep" to form a song; the song is made up of a group of sounds repeated at intervals and in a similar pattern. Nor is the song necessarily a vocal sound that comes out of a bird's mouth. Thus, both the rhythmic tapping of a woodpecker's beak and the drumming of a grouse with its wings (*page 52*) are songs. So are the sounds made by vibrating feathers in the aerial displays of the woodcock.

Birds make other sounds that cannot be called songs, but are known as calls. (A song is defined as a complicated, repeated pattern of sounds used to warn off a competing male or to attract a female. A call is defined as a short, sharp sound used to rally the flock or warn other birds of the presence of an enemy.) Both songs and calls are bird "talk"—they tell other birds something specific. The introduction of tape recorders has revolutionized the study of bird sounds.

Migrating birds often utter special "contact" notes, especially on night flights when the travelers may not be able to see one another. These special calls help the birds keep in contact as they fly through the sky. Many flocking birds also have special feeding notes, assembly signals and flight calls. On the fields where they graze, Canada geese talk in low, grunting notes. These birds signal a take-off with loud honking cries that swell into a continuous chorus during flight.

Every bird has a vocabulary dealing with food. All chicken raisers are familiar with the mother hen's excited food call that brings her young running toward her. A baby robin waiting for lunch signals its hunger by uttering light peeps that grow louder and

FALCON

DUMMY

GOOSE

A Dummy Spelling Danger

The dummy bird (*center*) has been used to show how chicks respond to danger. When it was pulled through the air short end frontward, it resembled a predatory falcon (*top*). Chicks froze in terror when they saw it. Pulled the other way, it looked like the harmless goose (*bottom*), and the chicks ignored it. It seemed that they feared the falcon image only because it was new; they had seen geese before and knew there was nothing to fear.

The Umbrellabird's Color and Song That Attract a Mate

The male umbrellabird of South America puts on a show of color when he sends out his strange, booming call. The bird spreads his rich crest of feathers like a canopy over his eyes and most of his beak (*near right*). Then to sound his call, the bird inflates a loose mass of wrinkled scarlet skin, tipped with a small feathery wattle. The result looks like a ripe tomato (*far right*).

louder as it gets hungrier and hungrier.

In certain instances, birds of different species seem to use sounds to cooperate with each other. For example, titmice, chickadees, woodpeckers and others often hunt for food in mixed groups. When one of these birds finds a food supply, it signals the find in such a way that all species in the group will understand. Different species do not really speak one another's language, but they seem to have a basic understanding of the other birds' sounds—at least where food is involved. This might be compared to an English-speaking person's ability to pick up a French newspaper and understand the major point of an article without being able to translate most of the minor details.

However, birds are more likely to compete for food than to share it. When a morsel is at stake they utter threatening cries or open their beaks as if ready to attack their neighbor. Usually a show of anger is enough, and the most determined-looking bird frightens off the others; occasionally, however, some birds actually fight with each other.

Another sound, the warning cry, is so important that birds often have different calls to signal different threats. A hen, spotting a hawk, utters a harsh squawk that sends chicks into hiding, but when a man approaches, the alarm is a cackling sound. The system of alarm signals is very important, for the approach of a bird of prey could mean sudden death to its victim. Even young birds hide at the sight of one. They seem to know, almost from birth, what their natural enemies look like and are ever watchful for signs of predators (*page 55*). But occasionally birds are fooled. Geese, for example, will often scatter when an airplane is sighted. They confuse it with their most powerful winged predator, the eagle, whose slow, stately flight resembles that of the airplane.

Of all the means birds use to talk to each other, the one that most delights man is the bird song, which sounds like a beautiful melody, but which is really the way one male threatens another; the more often the male sings his song, the more menacing his warning becomes.

What the singing bird is doing is telling all

Gaudily Decorated Bellbird:
Loudmouth of the Tropics

The South American bellbirds can be heard sounding their explosive notes half a mile away. Two species are seen here: the male bearded bellbird *(near right)* has a large cluster of stringy wattles hanging from his throat; the male three-wattled bellbird *(far right)* as his name suggests, has only three, but these swell up and lengthen when he calls. Both voice and strange wattles seem to attract females to the ardent males.

BEARDED BELLBIRD

other males that he is the owner of a piece of property—a feeding and nesting ground—where he shelters his mate and finds food for his young. Should the song of warning be ignored, the invading bird—who may be attempting to steal the mate by forcing the "homeowner" out—is attacked. Usually, however, the threat is enough to scare the challenger off.

Bold patterns, colors and other adornments are, like the vocal song, a form of communication. A rival male sees them as an invitation to battle—a warning to which he must respond either by fighting or by retreat. A female, on the other hand, sees the display as an invitation to mate—a sign that

the male is strong and determined, a suitable provider who will protect her.

Yet even for the female the male's song at first carries a threat. In response to his challenging attitude she indicates her non-aggressive and accepting attitude by some small gesture such as turning her head away or by acting like a baby and begging for food. By her special reaction he realizes that she is a female and therefore a likely mate. The male may then seal the bargain by transferring some delicious morsel from his bill to hers. This type of behavior is called courtship feeding.

The courtship rituals have more than one purpose. Sometimes members of closely related species look so similar that a bird has

58

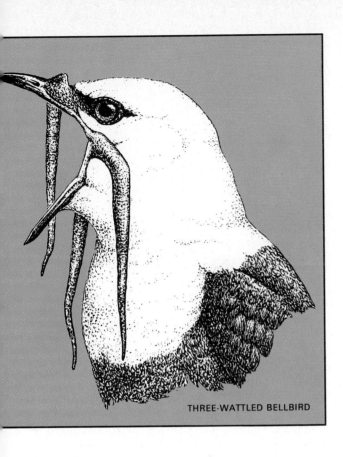

THREE-WATTLED BELLBIRD

difficulty in recognizing one of its own kind. In other cases, male and female birds of the same species are practically identical in appearance. Courtship rituals help birds to identify members of their own species and members of the opposite sex. The ritual of two closely related species of gulls (*pages 60 and 61*) is a good example of ceremonial display for purposes of identification.

Herons, too, have their own way of choosing mates from a crowd of birds that look almost exactly alike, though they may belong to several species. The male night heron, for instance, goes through a "song and dance" on his nest site. He extends his neck forward while stamping in place with his feet; then, dropping his head almost to the level of his feet, he utters a short *plup-buzz*. This display attracts females of the same species, and then the male can select a mate.

Some ceremonial displays are not only mating rites but are also competitive rituals. Wild male turkeys, called toms, proudly strut up and down in groups, their tails spread out like fans. They are paying more attention to each other than to the hens, for each tom is trying to prove himself more outstanding than his rivals. As the contest quickens. the toms become more excited and their naked heads turn blue while the sacs beneath their chins fill out with blood. When a hen is ready to mate, she must take the initiative by falling at the feet of the male of her

BLACK-HEADED GULL "LONG CALL" PATTERN

The Surprisingly Varied Patterns of the Gulls' Wedding March

Although they look much alike, two gull species—the black-headed gull *(near right)* and the little gull *(far right)*—can be identified by different motion patterns during the mating season. In the "long call" pattern *(top)*, both males call females; the black-headed gull stands straight, the little gull crouches. When a female responds *(center)*, the male and female black-headed gulls stare straight ahead in a forward pattern; little gulls greet each other by looking vertically upward. Finally, pairs of black-headed gulls face away from each other, while little gulls tilt their heads *(bottom)*.

FORWARD PATTERN

FACING-AWAY PATTERN

LITTLE GULL "LONG CALL" PATTERN

VERTICAL PATTERN

UPRIGHT PATTERN

choice. Only then will the tom halt his pompous and self-centered behavior.

In due time after birds have paired off, the female lays a clutch of eggs and hatches a family of hungry chicks. Feeding these tiny youngsters would seem to be an act so instinctive that signals between parent bird and chick would be unnecessary. In fact, if signals are not given, the nestlings will go hungry. European cuckoos, for example, lay their eggs, usually one at a time, in nests belonging to birds of other species. After a young cuckoo is hatched by its foster mother, it pushes out of the nest the baby birds that really belong there. Then, opening its bill wide, the cuckoo demands food. The foster parents, seeing the signal of the open bill, automatically stuff it with food and ignore their rightful children, which lie dying outside the nest. The adult birds are not cruel; they need the signal of the gaping mouth before they will feed a nestling, and since only the young cuckoo has the strength to give that sign, it gets the food. It is unlikely that the parents realize that the cuckoo is not their offspring.

Another way in which a young bird signals for food is by pecking at its mother's beak. A baby gull will peck at anything that resembles a beak, in the hope of getting food (*page 54*). Given this signal, the mother supplies a bit of fish.

All of these varied noises and actions are part of the birds' inborn language. This language differs not only from species to species,

MALE ROBINS

The Birds' Springtime Struggle for Living Space

Two male robins (*above*) fight; a male Baltimore oriole (*opposite*) sings. For each, hunting territories are at stake. The winning robin will take over a certain area. Then, like the oriole, he will sing to drive away other male robins; his song also attracts a female. As this view shows, territories of different species can overlap: eight pairs of robins (*brown lines*) and three pairs of orioles (*green lines*) share this ground.

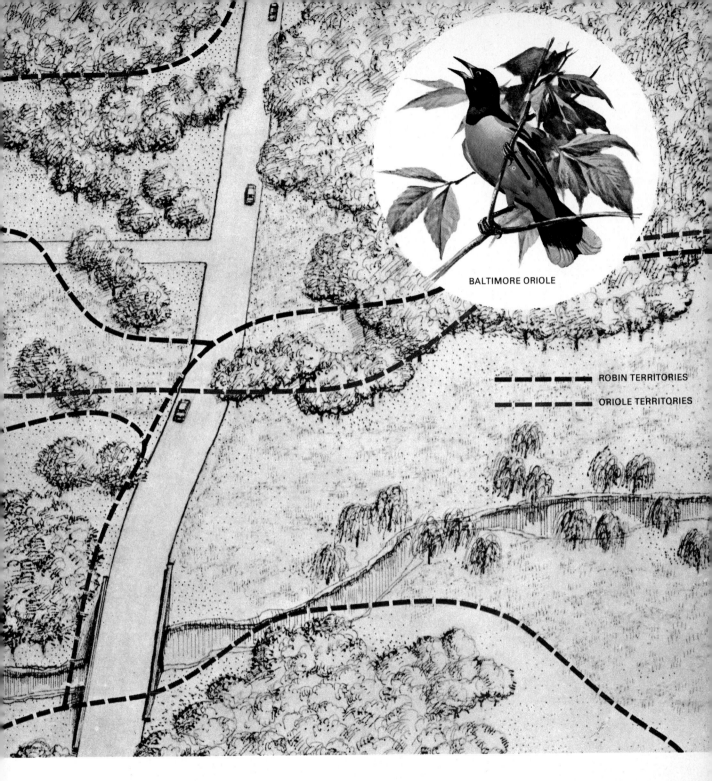

BALTIMORE ORIOLE

- - - - ROBIN TERRITORIES
- - - - ORIOLE TERRITORIES

but often—just as with human beings—it varies from "nation" to "nation." A recent experiment, for example, showed that French crows ignored the alarm call of American crows, apparently unable to understand it. As other pieces of similar information are collected, man moves steadily closer to the day when he may fully understand what the birds are saying when they "talk" to each other.

5

From Egg to Adult: Survival of the Fit

Within the temperate zones of the world, where the seasons come and go according to a pattern year after year, the first stirrings of new life among birds occur when winter gives way to early spring. Suddenly the birds seem irritable, slightly angry at one another. For the first time since autumn one can hear bits of bird songs—warnings issued by one male to another to stay away.

As the winter snows melt and the frozen soil softens, birds experience great physical changes that prepare them for reproduction and the raising of families. The time is at hand to lay claim to a territory and to build the nest where the eggs will be laid and kept safe and warm.

How does a bird select the site for its nest? After considerable searching, the male begins to return time and again to the same branch to sing his song of challenge. If no other male of his species replies, the bird has found a place. Now he must learn the limits of his territory. He may start with a plot of three or four acres, flitting from one singing post to another. But by the time he has gained complete control over a territory, it probably will be cut down to half that size as oth-

LARGEST AND SMALLEST EGGS found in the Western Hemisphere mark the beginning of a new generation of rheas *(left)* and hummingbirds. Inside, the growing embryo absorbs the whites, most of the yolk and part of the shell. The adult birds maintain the height difference shown by their eggs—about 10 to 1.

Man's Helping Hand for a Traditional Bird of Good Omen

European storks, the birds that folk-lore said carried human babies to their mothers, rest high on a church steeple (*right*). The number of these storks has been dropping, though no one knows why. They may have been killed by the insecticides on farms where they feed in the winter. Whatever the cause, the bird lovers of Alsace, where storks are considered good luck, are determined to rebuild the population. They are making nests for the storks, such as the one on the steeple at right, and have even imported stork eggs from North Africa and hatched them in incubators.

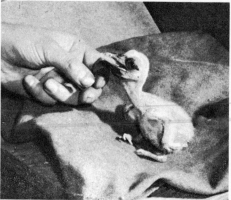

AN ALSATIAN BIRD LOVER carefully builds a nest (*left*) to attract storks. Another (*center*) feeds a chick that was hatched in an incubator. A sign (*right*) hung in restaurants of the area asks diners not to request frogs' legs, in order to conserve the favorite food of young storks, and is signed "The storks of Alsace."

er males of the species drive him away from the outlying sections—for they too are trying to define the limits of their domains.

When a male robin, for example, moves too far from his nesting site to sing his song, he will be challenged by his neighbor (*pages 62 and 63*) and forced to retreat closer to home. Should the second robin follow, the first will stand his ground, forcing the intruder away. Through this continuing vocal battle the birds discover how far afield they may go without invading another's territory.

A singing male is nearly always supreme within his own domain. Experiments have shown this to be so: a European robin, caged within his own territory, was able to frighten off intruders merely by singing. Similarly, a caged song sparrow was once placed within the territory of a neighboring sparrow. The confined bird went wild with fear. When the sparrow outside grabbed the caged sparrow's wing tip, the poor captive had a heart attack and fell dead.

Territory may be simply defined as any area a bird defends against its own kind. Its usefulness is that it spaces birds of one species fairly evenly over the land so that each family may have enough food to support it.

The amount of territory that each species needs varies widely. The American robin can make do with less than half an acre, but the male meadowlark requires up to 22 acres to support his family. A golden eagle may dominate an area of more than 35 square miles without competition from another male of the same species. Perhaps one reason why the ivory-billed woodpecker has become almost extinct is its feeding habits: each couple must have a territory of not less than six square miles of uncut swamp timber, a type of terrain that is rapidly disappearing. This same area could support 36 pairs of pileated woodpeckers or approximately 126 pairs of red-bellied woodpeckers.

There is no question that the availability of food has definite bearing on the size of a territory. When the spruce trees of Canada were attacked by budworm, the sudden increase in the number of insects made it possible for warblers to survive on a third of an acre per couple; they usually need somewhat more.

Some birds—usually those that feed on flying insects or schools of fish—gather in great colonies instead of staking out family claims. The primary requirement for a sea bird's survival is a nesting place safe from four-footed hunters; thus an island is ideal. Once found, such a refuge becomes the common property of all members of the flock. Sea birds catch fish and other marine or-

Two Fancy Woven Nests That Are Suspended for Safety

The elaborate hanging nests of the African weaverbird *(left)* and the South American oropendola *(right)* protect eggs from hungry monkeys and other enemies. The weaverbird, one of the world's best nest builders, can hold down a grass strand with its foot while fastening the other end with its beak, as shown; it may use as many as 300 strands to make the loose, hollow nest that swings from a branch or leaf. The female crested oropendola weaves her nest of leaf fibers and vine stems by herself. Males have nothing to do with nest building or with raising the family.

ganisms for food. Thus, they can choose as a roost any rocky shoal; they do not rely on the land for their food.

Birds that share nesting grounds must cooperate with one another. Family territory is reduced to the nest itself—or to the distance a bird can strike with its beak while sitting on its eggs. On Isla Raza in the Gulf of California, more than 40,000 terns nest on an acre of soil—one bird per square foot.

The nesting practices of land birds vary greatly. For example, some species arrive at their nesting areas in great flocks, but robins show up in the northern United States over a period of two months. Earliest on the scene are the stray birds, hopeful of gaining terri-

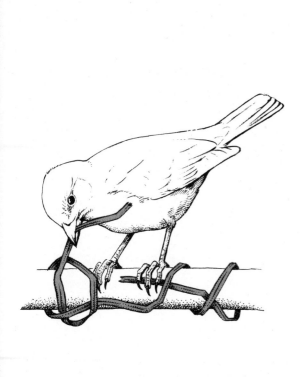

tories before competition arrives. Next come numbers of adult males, which claim territories they may have held the year before; then come the females. Finally the young males arrive and seek out territories wherever they can.

Among nearly all land birds, vacant territories are quickly filled; there always seem to be more than enough males ready to mate. In New Jersey some years ago a male indigo bunting was captured after he had mated. By next morning the female had taken a new mate. Nine times in as many days the males were removed—each time to be replaced by a new partner.

Once couples have paired off they are ready to produce a family. Most songbirds and ducks are capable of mating before the first birthday. Herring gulls, however, take at least three years to reach maturity; eagles take four or five. Certain sea birds take the longest of all: an albatross does not mate until it is skilled enough at catching seafood to provide for its offspring—perhaps five to seven years.

The building of a nest is closely tied to courtship and mating. In fact, the nest may be constructed as part of the ritual of courtship. A female tern, for example, pivots on her breast to face the male, who circles about her. The swiveling movements create a saucerlike depression in the sand. Some tern species lay their eggs in this depression without further ado.

Most other birds build nests after mating. To begin with, the bird squats in a clump of grass, punching or molding it with its body, or it tries to fit itself into a likely fork between two branches of a tree or shrub. A few twigs are pushed into place; if they do not stick, the bird will try another site. In time, by tucking, poking, pushing and molding scraps of twigs, grass and other materials, the bird shapes a cuplike home.

No two species build identical nests. An expert observer can often identify a bird merely by examining the nest; the building materials, size, structure and location are all clues. Nests vary widely in complexity. Some whippoorwill-like birds lay their well-camouflaged eggs on the bare ground; orioles construct exquisitely woven purselike structures. Most intricate of all is the complicated basketry of weaverbirds (*pages 68 and 69*).

Some birds' nests are extremely small. As might be expected, the hummingbird builds one of the tiniest, scarcely an inch in diameter. Equally small is the saucer of bark, down feathers and dried glue in which the crested tree swift lays its single egg. On the other hand, a bald eagle's nest found in Vermilion, Ohio, measured eight and a half feet in diameter, was 12 feet deep and weighed about two tons. Even larger are the nests of megapodes, strange Australian fowl that do not use their body heat to hatch their eggs. Instead they pile up great mounds of vegetation; the rotting material gives off heat to keep the eggs warm. One species of megapode, the scrub fowl, builds mounds that sometimes reach 20 feet in height and cover an area about 50 feet across.

Besides differing widely in size, nests display a variety of architectural styles. Woodpeckers drill out their nurseries in the trunks of trees and lay their eggs inside on beds of

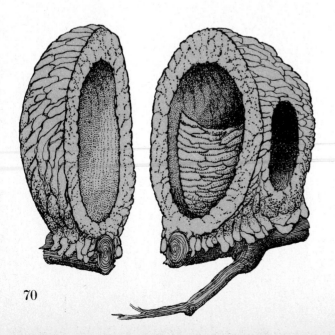

Birds That Build Fortresses for Their Fragile Eggs

The nests of the rufous ovenbird of South America (*left*) and of the African silvery-cheeked hornbill (*right*) are practically small forts. The ovenbird builds a nest of cemented sand so strong it will not crack even if a rock is thrown at it. Inside, the eggs are protected by a wall between the entrance and the nest. The male hornbill walls the female in a hollow tree for three months until the chicks are grown; by then, she—fed by him—is fat and barely able to fly.

wood chips. After the woodpecker's mating season ends, the vacant apartments are taken over by titmice, wrens, flycatchers, swallows and bluebirds. They remodel the rooms, bringing twigs and grass to feather their pre-constructed nests.

The open-topped bowl typical of many land birds may be deep and soft inside like the nest of a goldfinch or shallow and twiggy like a dove's. Others are firmly woven of grass and hair, like a warbler's home. The American robin strengthens its nest by cementing its walls with mud; vireos and chaffinches bind theirs together with cobwebs.

While some nests are built at ground level,

Parrots That Tunnel in Mounds

Although most parrots nest in hollow trees, the paradise parrot (*below*) and other Australian and New Guinea parrots have learned how to dig into termite mounds and hollow out their nesting chamber inside. Shown here is a male next to the entrance he has made, and a female inside incubating her eggs. The nest is lined with material taken from the termite tunnels.

others may be found 100 feet or more up in the tallest trees; most are within six or eight feet of the ground. The nests of most small birds are built in a week's time. A song sparrow in a hurry to mate can finish a nest— and an excellent one too—in as little as three days.

Though no bird lays its eggs in the water, grebes come close to it, depositing theirs on small pieces of floating debris or vegetation drifting in a marsh. When the grebe leaves the exposed eggs and slips into the water, it will often blanket the unhatched chicks with vegetation. This both conceals the eggs and keeps them warm. Ducks accomplish the same thing by wrapping their eggs in a

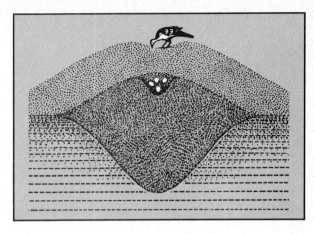

A Father That Tends the Nest

The Australian mallee fowl (*below*) uses the heat of decaying plant material to incubate its eggs. The eggs are placed in a huge pile of rotting leaves and trash (*above*) collected by the male bird and covered with a layer of sand. The male then tests the temperature inside the nest with his beak, adding or taking away sand to keep it at a temperature from 90° to 96° F.

PUFFINS

MURRES

RAZOR-BILLED AUK

BLACK GUILLEMOT

74

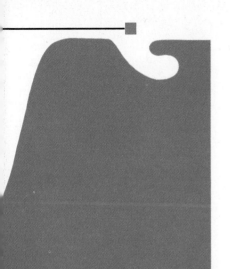

A High-Rise Apartment House for Four Families of Auks

From Maine to Labrador, millions of sea birds nest each spring on seaside cliffs, like the one diagramed at left, and offshore islands. The various kinds of auks divide nesting places on the cliff according to species. Puffins build their nests at the top in burrows dug in the ground. Murres lay their tapered eggs on the bare rock of a ledge. The razor-billed auk finds shelter in a crevice or overhang. At the bottom, the black guillemot nests on pebbles under loose rocks.

quilt of fluffy down from their own breasts.

Mud is a useful nest-building material. Flamingos make cone-shaped mounds of mud, sometimes over a foot high. The bird shapes mud into pellets and then builds the nest, pellet by pellet. Cliff swallows and house martins fasten jug-shaped nests of mud under ledges, bridges and eaves. The rufous ovenbird of Argentina gets part of its name from the nest it builds *(page 70)*. The bird mixes sand and cow dung into a building material that it shapes into a ball-like structure. As the nest dries, it becomes rock-hard and its shape resembles that of an old-fashioned oven.

Among the most skilled nestbuilders are those that suspend their homes. The vireos of North America weave firm little baskets, hanging them from the forks of twigs. The nests of orioles, swinging from the tip ends of slender branches, are deeper— and their relatives, the oropendolas of the American tropics, knit nests that look like

(Text continued on page 78)

GREAT HORNED OWL

BLACK SKIMMER

COMMON MURRE

COMMON SNIPE

BALTIMORE ORIOLE

AMERICAN COOT

SCRUB FOWL

EMU

SNOWY EGRET

CARDINAL

GUIRA CUCKOO

ROBIN

NORTH ISLAND KIWI

CRESTED TINAMOU

BROAD-BILLED HUMMINGBIRD

JACANA

COMMON CROW

NEW GUINEA MANUCODE
(BIRD OF PARADISE)

WHITE PELICAN

Eggs of All Sizes and Shapes, Colors and Textures

The largest known egg belonged to the extinct elephant bird; it held more than two gallons. Its size is shown here as a white outline behind a selection of eggs of living birds, all shown in actual size. Usually, the larger the bird, the larger its egg, but this is not always true. The kiwi, less than half the size of the white pelican, has an egg almost twice as long. In fact, the kiwi's egg is the largest in relation to the size of the bird. This explains its long shape; if it were rounder, the female could not lay it. Eggs like the murre's, which are laid on sea ledges, are often tapered. If they roll, they roll in tight circles and do not fall off (page 74). The colors seem to mean little, except that spots help hide eggs laid on the ground. White eggs often belong to birds that nest in holes or burrows—where they are hidden anyway.

Two Chicks, Feathered and Not, on Their First Day of Life

At birth, most birds are helpless, blind and naked. The sorry-looking, day-old meadowlark chick *(top)* cannot leave its nest for 10 to 12 days. A few birds, however, can fend for themselves just after hatching. One of these, the killdeer *(bottom)*, may run and feed itself hours after it has broken out of its shell.

three-foot-long socks. Twenty or 30 such bags may dangle from a single ceiba tree. Some weavers build a very complex hanging nest that is entered through a dangling sleeve below the circular nesting chamber. A guard rail inside the chamber keeps the eggs from falling through the sleeve.

The great problem in building hanging nests is, of course, how to attach them. The Australian rock warbler, which hangs its frail nest from the roof of a cave, uses sticky spider webs as glue. The weaverbirds of Africa and southern Asia actually tie knots. The ultimate in simplicity of suspension is achieved by the green broadbill of Malaya, which hangs its complex woven nest over a woodland pool by means of one long string wrapped around an overhanging bough.

Most complex nest designs developed as an aid to survival. The hanging nest is most often seen in the tropics, where its design makes it difficult for monkeys to steal eggs. Some birds build nests near colonies of hornets and other stinging or biting insects, which may help guard them from predators.

Few birds construct stranger nests than the swifts. Most of the 76 species of swifts use their saliva, which hardens into a rocklike material, to bind their nests together. The swallow-tailed swifts of tropical America use saliva and feathers to build soft feltlike tubes. These nests—often up to two feet long—dangle beneath rocky shelves. The palm swift of Africa glues its two eggs upright on a feltlike pad stuck onto a drooping palm leaf. Even if the leaf is turned upside down in a storm, the eggs stick.

Certain cave swiftlets of Asia build little saucers entirely of saliva. Tremendous numbers of these birds colonize limestone caverns. In Indochina, workers with long poles knock down the nests and collect them to make a delicious dish called bird's-nest soup *(page 118)*.

Most penguins nest in burrows, but the emperor penguin, largest of the family, needs no nest at all. Its single youngster per year is hatched in the dead of the antarctic winter when the temperature sometimes drops to 40° F. below zero. After the female lays her egg, the male takes over. He places the egg on top of his feet, over which the warm

MEADOWLARK

KILLDEER

skin and feathers of his belly sag to form a protective blanket. Bracing himself against the cold winds and gaining some warmth from fellow penguins who crowd close to him, the father patiently warms the egg for more than two months until the chick hatches. He will have lost 25 of his 75 pounds before the well-fed female slides in at last to relieve him and feed the newborn chick.

The huddling of penguins is not the only example of how birds cooperate in keeping an egg warm or in nesting. The hanging nest of the South African weaver is a regular apartment house, so large that at a distance it might be mistaken for a human hut. More than 100 pairs of weavers may build nests in the haystacklike structure.

The laying of eggs is timed to coincide with the completion of the nest; it may begin as soon as the day after the last stick or straw has been pushed into its place. Some birds, however, take a breather for several days before beginning to lay eggs. Among the perching birds the usual rate is one egg every day, laid in the morning. The cuckoo outwits its neighbors by sneaking in during the afternoon to lay its own egg in another bird's nest.

The number of eggs a bird lays may be keyed to its life expectancy, its enemies and the other problems it faces. Hummingbirds, with few enemies, lay only two eggs during the nesting season; wrens, with a shorter life span and more enemies, rear two families per summer of six or seven chicks each.

As might be expected, the tiniest egg is that of the hummingbird (*page 64*). The largest is that of the ostrich; it is five to seven inches long, has a very thick shell and would take about 40 minutes to hard-boil.

Tiny birds with a tendency to reproduce in large numbers may lay a single group of eggs heavier than the mother's own body weight. Among this group are some of the titmice, the kinglets and the goldcrests. A ruddy duck may weigh scarcely more than a pound, but its average clutch of nine eggs weighs nearly twice as much.

Do birds recognize their own eggs? Nobody is sure. In a colony of terns the patterns on the shells vary from tiny specks to large blotches. Since terns often nest only a beak's reach away from one another, egg recognition might be thought important to them. However, experiments show that even in such crowded circumstances it is the nest site rather than the egg that attracts the bird. A tern will attempt to hatch even a flash bulb if it is in the right place. On the other hand, when a sooty tern, which lays only one egg, was given a choice of two, it usually sat on its own egg.

Nearly 80 species of birds are completely parasitic at nesting time. This means that

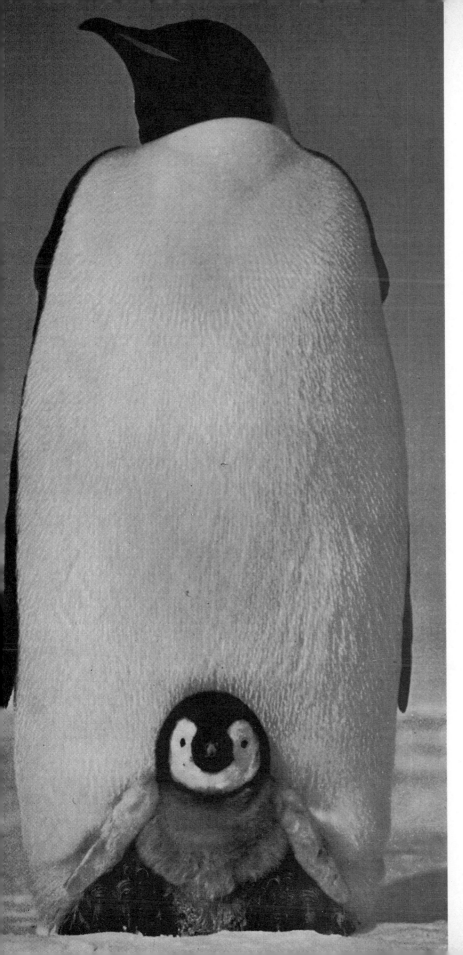

A Warm Home for a Baby Emperor on a Parent's Feet

A baby emperor penguin peers out from its snug home under its parent's warm fold of skin. Largest of the penguin family, the emperor has no nest. For more than two months, the father keeps the egg warm in the antarctic cold, most severe on earth. Then the baby spends weeks riding about on its father's or mother's large feet.

Early Days of Life and Growth in the Eagle's Nest

The golden eagle spends its first few weeks in a nest on the side of a cliff, safe from all enemies except man. The newly hatched eaglet *(left)*, downy and helpless, weighs only three ounces. In four weeks the eaglet *(above)*, whose crop bulges from a recent feeding, weighs 46 ounces and has begun to sprout wings. Six weeks old, the five-pound youngster *(below)* wanders on ledges, but it cannot fly for six more weeks.

they lay their eggs in the nests of other species, leaving the care of their young to foster parents. A number of other species are part-time parasites. They will usually build their own nests and care for their young but will occasionally lay eggs in other nests. Among North American ducks, more than 20 species sometimes lay eggs in their neighbors' nests; one, the redhead, often does so.

The most famous of all parasitic birds is the cuckoo of Europe and Asia. The cuckoo is the uninvited guest in the nests of at least 300 species. To make room for itself in a small nest, the young cuckoo squirms and shoves until its nestmates—the rightful inhabitants—are heaved overboard.

In the New World, cowbirds are the principal parasites. Each young cowbird hatched in the nest of another species pushes out one or two of its host's own young.

Some birds lay the same number of eggs each breeding season; others lay varying numbers. Some, such as sandpipers and plovers, which usually lay four eggs, will not lay another if one is stolen or lost. Others keep on laying if their eggs disappear; one flicker, whose single egg was removed from the nest each day, laid 71 eggs in 73 days; a European wryneck laid 62 eggs in 62 days. Domestic fowl, to the delight of chicken and duck raisers, will continue to lay eggs as fast as they disappear from the nest. The record for a chicken is 361 eggs in a year. A duck did even better, laying 363 eggs in 365 days.

Merely sitting on eggs does not guarantee

A Protected Nest in the City for a Threatened Bird

This family of whooping cranes, a bird on the brink of extinction, has set up housekeeping in the paddock of the New Orleans Audubon Park Zoo. At left, a one-day-old crane is fed insects by its parents. When

the bird that they will hatch. The eggs must be kept at a relatively warm and even temperature. Since feathers can interfere with the passing of body heat to the eggs, most birds develop "brood spots," patches on the underbody where the feathers have fallen out, allowing the eggs to rest against the warm skin. A bird may have as many as three brood spots; if both parents share the job of hatching eggs, both have brood spots.

Eggs need not be covered all the time. Although the temperature of an egg is maintained in the low 90s, the developing bird inside is more likely to be killed by too much

full grown, its diet will include worms, snakes and shellfish. The six-week-old baby at right, awkward on stiltlike legs, may grow to be more than five feet tall. As an adult, its loud cry will be heard for two miles.

heat than by too little. Among many perching birds, the female, which is solely responsible for brooding, will take a 6- to 10-minute break from her motherly duties every half hour or so.

The time needed to hatch an egg—the incubation period—varies widely from species to species. In some perching birds the young are born after only 11 days, but among kiwis and albatrosses incubation may take as long as 80 days. The longest period of incubation known to man was that of a mallee fowl. Ninety days went by between the laying of the egg and the birth of the chick; normally the incubation period for this species is only 62 days.

When a baby bird is ready to be born it must break out of the egg, an action called pipping. So that the creature can free itself from its prison, it is equipped with an "egg tooth," a small growth on the upper bill used to chip away at the egg shell. This growth is a remnant of the birds' reptilian ancestry; snakes and lizards also have egg teeth. But these teeth disappear from all three creatures soon after birth.

The young birds fall into two main groups. Most birds belong to the group called altricial. This means that they have spent only a relatively short time in the egg, so that they are born before reaching an advanced state of physical development. They emerge blind, featherless and feeble, unable to do much more than open their mouths for food.

The second category, called precocial, applies to chicks that have spent at least 24 to 28 days in the egg. Precocial birds emerge from the egg bright-eyed, fully feathered and able to run after their parents and peck at things as soon as their down dries.

Oddly enough, the altricial bird reaches adulthood faster than the precocial bird. A young songbird, born naked and helpless, eats and grows at a furious rate. A European cuckoo may weigh only two grams at birth;

Pelican Families and Their Nests with an Ocean View

At home by the sea, brown pelicans approach their shallow nests in a bird sanctuary near Cape Romaine, South Carolina. Adult pelicans feed their demanding nestlings by catching fish in the nearby lagoon. By the time the pelican chicks are old enough to fly, each one will have eaten more than 150 pounds of food.

three weeks later it weighs 50 times as much.

If the young can be called growth machines, the parents are feeding machines, constantly forced to hunt for food with which to appease their chicks. A pair of phoebes was reported to have made 845 trips to the nest in a single day. An eagle, on the other hand, may make only two or three trips daily, but the food it brings back will serve its young for many meals.

When a bird leaves the nest to strike out on its own, it is said to be "fledged." For the warbler this occurs only nine days after birth, but the albatross, at the other extreme, does not make its first flight to sea until it is six months old. The first few months of a bird's independent existence will prove its capacity for survival. Many birds do not live to see their first birthday; they are just not efficient enough to compete for food or survive wind, rain, cold and disease.

When the next breeding season starts there should, in theory, be just about the same number of bird pairs as there were the year before. By permitting an excess number of birds to be born and then weeding out the weakest, nature keeps a balance between the food supply and the bird population. At the same time nature, by testing each bird, assures the "survival of the fittest" and a healthy breeding stock for the future.

6

The Steady Struggle to Stay Well Fed

Nearly every variety of animal and plant on earth helps feed some species of bird. The remains of whales and elephants become food for gulls and vultures. At the other end of the scale, one of the tiniest of all plants, blue-green alga, is the main source of food for the three million or so lesser flamingos that crowd the great salt lakes of East Africa. In fact, one of the reasons why these birds, among the most ancient of living species, still exist is that they can support themselves on a diet that would appeal to few other creatures.

The unique menu on which the lesser flamingo thrives helps explain a rather complicated biological idea—that of niche. A bird's niche is its place in the world, and the success each species has in adapting to that place determines whether it will prosper or die off. The lesser flamingo prospers be-

FEEDING ON A MAGPIE, the prairie falcon makes a meal of a favorite prey. But as an example of nature's complicated checks and balances, if the falcon stays away from its nest too long, it may lose its eggs to another hungry magpie. In the spring, the falcon also feeds its young on ground squirrels and other rodents.

| OWL | SPARROW | WOODCOCK |

Eyes Front, Side and Back for Hunting Hidden Prey

The position of these birds' eyes serves their special feeding habits. Each bird can see everything within the shaded areas; where these areas overlap *(dark)*, they can also judge distance. With eyes forward, owls can follow moving prey. Sparrows' eyes, on the side, can spot danger, yet see forward well enough to find seeds. Woodcock, which feed in mud, have eyes set to the rear so they can watch for danger while eating.

cause it lives beside a plentiful source of blue-green alga and has no competition for this food supply.

Almost every part of the world—the forests, mountains, grasslands, scrub, marshes, deserts, tundra, rivers, lakes, islands, seas and lately the cities and farms—has its own birds. They have developed along with the food available in the various places. A bird finds its niche in a specific area not by accident, but by a process of natural selection— nature's way of killing off the weak and unsuitable and permitting the survival of those individuals and species that can better adapt to local conditions.

Insect-eating birds, for example, reveal the complex ways in which natural selection maintains a balance between various forms of life. It is often said that were it not for the birds, insects would overrun the earth. This is an exaggeration because insects

face a variety of dangers besides birds. It is true that birds do a great deal to hold down the numbers of insects. Warblers and other migrants arrive at their feeding grounds at precisely the time when billions of small insect eggs are hatching. The birds gather up these larval insects to nourish their own hungry young. Baby birds eat nearly their own weight in insects every day; adult birds need comparatively less food, yet some full-grown insect eaters consume as much as four tenths of their weight daily.

Insects, no matter where they live, are hard put to escape from birds that turn over leaves, strip bark from trees and peer at every twig. There is a bird of some kind that hunts and eats nearly every kind of insect. Warblers and vireos search them out from their hiding places among leaves. Swallows and swifts spend most of their waking hours on the wing, traveling hundreds of miles

Protection for the Hunted, All Alone and in a Group

The ptarmigan in summer plumage *(above)* and the bobwhite quail in a huddle *(below)* show two ways birds protect themselves from their enemies. The ptarmigan, with its spotted feathers, becomes almost invisible against the landscape. The quail's circle serves two purposes: like western pioneers settled for the night, all keep a lookout for danger; and together they stay warm during the autumn and winter nights.

daily in their never-ending quest for air-borne insects.

In tropical America a number of species follow swarms of army ants, to feed on the other insects that scramble from their concealment before the onslaught of the ant hordes. Similarly, in Africa, when native tribesmen set grass fires to improve the land for cattle raising, birds are quick to take advantage of the situation. The fires expose colonies of insects; the ground hornbills stalk close to the cooling grass, while kestrels hover in the smoke, ready to swoop down and scoop up dinner.

Grazing animals also flush insects from their hide-outs, and such birds as bustards, cattle egrets and bee eaters follow on the heels of zebras, cattle and antelope to benefit from this process. As the four-legged creatures pass by, the birds flock behind them to devour millions of insects roused into flight by the passing herd.

Many birds hunt insects in the trunks of trees. These include the nuthatches, creepers, woodcreepers and some wood warblers; but none are as well equipped for the job as the woodpeckers (*pages 94 and 95*). These birds spend most of their lives clamped against a trunk or a branch, their stiff tails acting as a support and their deeply curved claws clutching the rough bark. A woodpecker has a straight beak that is as hard as steel. Powerful muscles in the head and neck drive the beak, as if it were a miniature jackhammer, into a tree. When insects in-

The Blurred Vision of Man

A distant object, here a rabbit *(below)*, appears as little more than a blur when seen by a man. A hawk, on the other hand, sees the rabbit in clear detail *(opposite page)*. In both man and hawk, the image is received in the eye by the retina, a layer of light-sensitive cells. In man's eye, the most sensitive spot (the macular area) is a cluster of some 200,000 such cells.

A RABBIT AS SEEN BY A MAN

RETINA

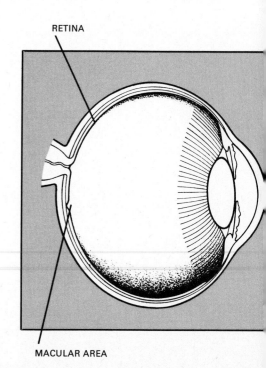

MACULAR AREA

festing a tree trunk are uncovered by a woodpecker, the bird's flexible tongue flashes into the hole to snare a meal.

On the Galápagos Islands one species of finch has adopted the woodpecker's technique. Though its beak retains the cone shape of a seedeater, the woodpecker finch manages to feed like a woodpecker by using a cactus needle as a drill. Picking up the needle with its bill, it pokes the spear into the tiny holes made by insects and stabs one with the sharp point, much as a human being might pick up a small piece of meat with a toothpick. The woodpecker finch is believed to be the only bird that makes use of a tool to get its food.

In the beginning of their evolutionary history all birds probably ate small animals such as insects. Seed eating is almost certainly a later development. Even today, nearly all seed-eating birds start their newly hatched young on a diet of insects and then slowly switch them over to a vegetarian way of life. Pigeons are an exception. They start their young on a diet of "pigeon's milk," a fluid that comes from both parents' bodies.

The rise of seed-eating birds must have occurred fairly recently, at least in terms of the many millions of years of bird life. Most seedeaters probably developed during the same geological period as grasses and marsh plants—in the last 13 million years.

Seed eating is common in several orders of birds, but it is among the various perching birds that the strong, cone-shaped bill that is

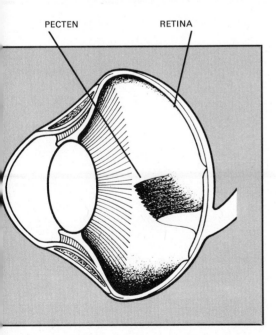

PECTEN   RETINA

The Keen Eye of the Hawk

Hawks see better than men because their eyes have more visual cells to fill in details (*below*). In the hawk's eye the sensitive spots (the foveae) contain one and a half million cells, eight times as many as man. The hawk's eye has a ridge, the pecten, to supply extra blood. This pecten may cast shadows on the retina, which help the bird see distant movements.

A RABBIT AS SEEN BY A HAWK

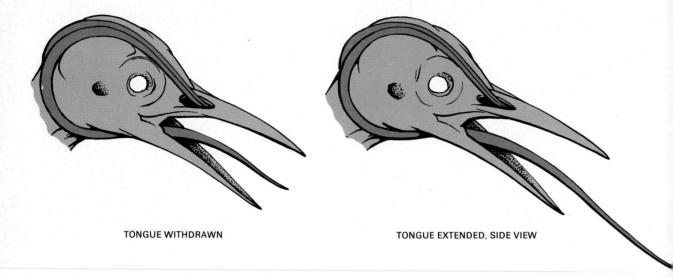

TONGUE WITHDRAWN   TONGUE EXTENDED, SIDE VIEW

designed for seed cracking is found. Such a bill is typical of finches and buntings; many experts believe these to be among the most recently developed birds.

Roots, grass, leaves, buds, seeds, fruit pulp, nectar, pollen and sap of various plants find their way into the diet of birds. Nectar, the sweet liquid manufactured by many flowering plants from which bees make honey, is a staple in the diet of nearly one fifth of all the world's birds. A bird watcher in New England knows that the ruby-throated hummingbird lives on nectar and that Baltimore orioles sometimes poke at blossoms. But, surprisingly, another 1,600 species on five continents are also nectar feeders.

Most nectar eaters live in the southern half of the world. The hummingbirds, a rainbow-colored family of about 320 species, are the most efficient of all nectar gatherers. They hover like miniature helicopters before flowers, probing them deftly with needlelike bills to sip up the nectar. The tiniest hum-

mingbird, the bee hummingbird of Cuba, is only two and a quarter inches long, smaller than some of the sphinx moths—insects these little birds closely resemble in shape, wing length and wing action.

Small though it is, the amount of energy burned up by a hummer is extraordinary. If a 170-pound man were to work as hard as the ruby-throated hummingbird he would need to eat 285 pounds of hamburger or 340 pounds of potatoes every day to stay alive.

In spite of their strong powers of flight hummingbirds have never crossed the Atlantic. However, a large family of Old World birds, the sunbirds, numbering more than 100 species, attempts to fill the flower niche in the Old World. Most are only a little larger than the hummingbirds, and many are just as colorful. But they cannot compare with hummingbirds in flying skill; they must perch while they sip and only rarely do they hover before a blossom.

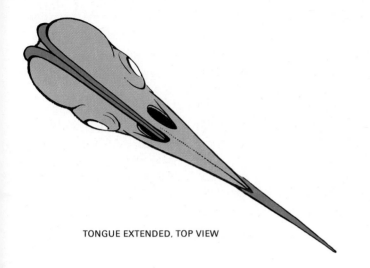

TONGUE EXTENDED, TOP VIEW

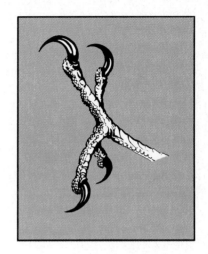

Nectar feeders must be travelers, able to follow the blossoming flowers from south to north or from lowlands to highlands. Hawaiian honey creepers travel in loose flocks from one section of the forest to another, their movements dictated by the blooming of the ohia, mamane and other native trees. Hummingbirds in the western United States migrate through the Pacific lowlands when the early spring flowers are at their best, but must go up to the high mountain meadows in late summer when the valleys lie parched and brown.

A branch of the parrot family, the lorikeets, which lives in Australia and parts of Asia, is also a nectar feeder, but the lorikeet goes about its work in a much cruder fashion than the hummingbird. Instead of delicately sipping the honeyed liquid from blossoms, the lorikeet crushes the bristly petals of the eucalyptus to sop up the sticky juices with its fringe-tipped tongue. Like other parrots, the lorikeet enjoys company and travels

Two Fancy Features That Help the Woodpecker to Peck Wood

The woodpecker's equipment for getting food includes a four-toed foot (*above*) and a flexible tongue. To hold on as it pecks, the bird uses two toes at the back of its foot for braces; most birds have only one toe there. After drilling a hole the woodpecker extends its tongue and pulls out grubs. The tongue, along with its connecting tissue (*above left and opposite*), loops under the jaw, around the head and ends in a nostril.

Eating on the Fly: A Skimmer's Trap For Catching Fish

A black skimmer picks up small fish by plowing the water with its lower bill. This wide ranging bird, found from New York to Burma, is a relative of the gulls and puffins. Its long bill is ideally suited for fishing on the wing. But bills can be put to uses other than feeding. Hornbills use theirs for defense, and toucans show off with theirs during courtship.

the mountain forests in large gangs, which settle down where the blossoms are thickest. Twittering and chattering all the while, the lorikeets pause briefly to decorate a tree with their brilliant colors, then they rush away in search of juicier blossoms.

Tropical fruit-eating birds, like the nectar feeders, are usually bedecked with brilliant feathers, and most of these birds are noisy. Parrots fly in pairs or flocks over the tropical forests, shrieking loudly. After finding a heavily laden tree, the parrots signal the treasure to flocks flying overhead, inviting their cousins to share a banquet. This kind of cooperation works to benefit all, for a tree heavy with ripening fruit may be difficult to find in the dark jungle. By sharing good fortune each bird is able to spend more time eating and less time searching for food.

Much more subdued than most tropical birds are the soft-voiced waxwings, sleek, crested birds dressed in muted browns and grays. Cedar waxwings may winter as far north as southern Canada, but they also fly as far south as Panama, traveling in tight flocks and lingering only when they find a treeful of berries. The bird watcher cannot predict their arrivals and departures, for they stay in a neighborhood only as long as the fruit lasts. Thus the Bohemian waxwing will be found in Scandinavia as long as the rowan tree has fruit, but when the berries give out, it may cross the North Sea to invade England.

Sometimes food is not to be found however patiently a bird searches. On occasion, when a blight kills off their favorite food, land birds may go hungry. Sea birds, on the other hand, seldom want for food.

Five sevenths of the earth's surface is covered by salt water, yet the birds that search the seas for food make up only three per cent of the world's species. There are only about 260 species of sea birds, and 110 of these, like gulls, terns, frigate birds and pelicans, stick close to the coasts.

While the seas abound in food, it is not evenly distributed throughout. Plankton—the tiny, floating sea organisms on which small fish feed—are found mostly in cool waters. Small fish are prey to larger fish, which in turn are the food of many sea birds. Therefore sea birds are much more numerous in areas where cold ocean currents favor the growth of plankton.

One of the places most crowded with sea birds is the cold Humboldt Current off the coast of Peru. Cormorants, piqueros and pelicans are attracted to this area. The fishing is so fine in these waters that one expert has estimated that the birds there catch about the same weight in fish as all the commercial fishermen in the United States.

Besides the 260 species classified as sea birds, there are fully 600 others that might be called water birds. These are the species that live in lakes, swamps and marshes. Some of these, like the scoters, eiders, grebes

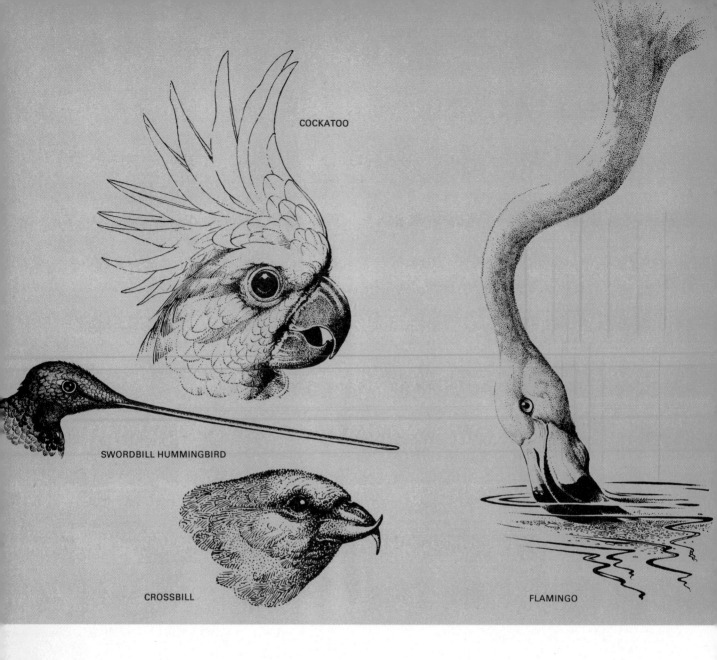

COCKATOO

SWORDBILL HUMMINGBIRD

CROSSBILL

FLAMINGO

and loons, sometimes are sea birds—ranging far out into the ocean—for part of the year.

Loons are among the very few birds with solid, heavy bones. This physical trait means that they do not float easily on water—which is a great help to a bird that spends much time diving deep below the water's surface to seek out fish. One loon was snared in a fisherman's net 240 feet deep in the water. Both loons and grebes are poorly suited for walking on land. So uncomfortable are

they on land that they avoid taking their feet out of the water, except for flying, for months on end.

The long-legged "glamor birds," the herons, storks, ibises, spoonbills and cranes, numbering about 120 species, are marsh inhabitants. They hunt fish, frogs, small reptiles, shellfish and large insects. Their stilt-like legs carry them high above the water, and their long necks permit them to reach

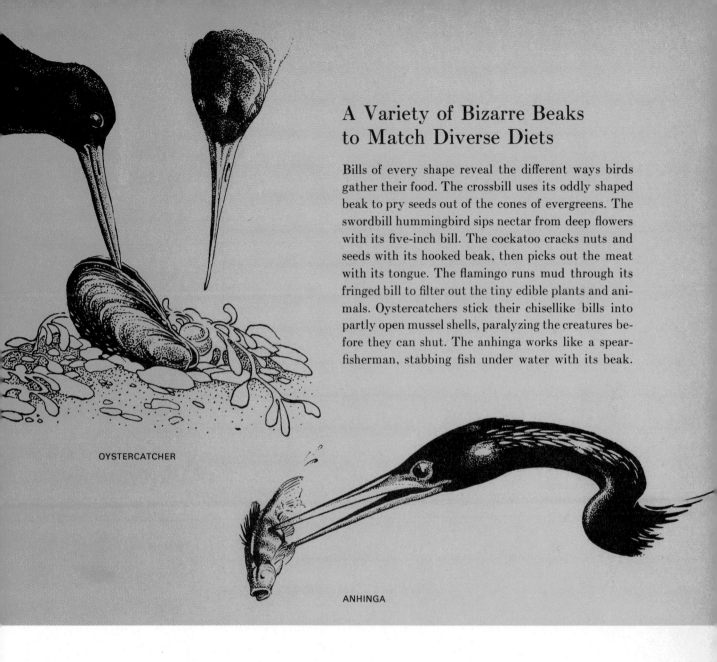

A Variety of Bizarre Beaks
to Match Diverse Diets

Bills of every shape reveal the different ways birds gather their food. The crossbill uses its oddly shaped beak to pry seeds out of the cones of evergreens. The swordbill hummingbird sips nectar from deep flowers with its five-inch bill. The cockatoo cracks nuts and seeds with its hooked beak, then picks out the meat with its tongue. The flamingo runs mud through its fringed bill to filter out the tiny edible plants and animals. Oystercatchers stick their chisellike bills into partly open mussel shells, paralyzing the creatures before they can shut. The anhinga works like a spearfisherman, stabbing fish under water with its beak.

OYSTERCATCHER

ANHINGA

down to scoop up a morsel from below the surface (*pages 100 and 101*).

The smaller waders, the snipe, sandpipers, plovers and their relatives, denied access to deeper water, concentrate along the shoreline, where they catch sand fleas, probe for marine worms, eat mosquito young, take small crabs or knock limpets off rocks. If it can be eaten, there is a wader to eat it.

In their feeding habits—and in every other behavior pattern—birds are a constant reminder of one fact of evolution: that every species has developed along with its surroundings. Each bird not only takes from its territory; it also gives something to it. Fishermen have often found that they can make their best catches if they stand downstream from a group of herons. The nitrogen-rich droppings of the birds enrich the water, fish multiply and the herons—and fishermen— prosper on the abundance of fish. A hunter who brings down a duck may notice tiny oval leaves sticking to its feathers. This is duckweed. All marsh ducks eat these leaves. As the ducks fly from pond to pond they carry the leaves with them. When they settle down in the water, the leaves float off, take root and begin to multiply. In this way duckweed survives and marsh ducks prosper by harvesting new crops of the plant, crops that the ducks themselves have sown.

Some of the most dramatic feeding habits are displayed by the birds of prey, some 400 species strong. Two thirds of their number—the hawks, eagles, falcons and vultures —hunt by day. The others, mostly species of owls, fly by night. In North America the great horned owl comes out at dusk to prowl the same area over which the hawk soared at noon. The owls' huge eyes can see in the dim-mest light, and their acute ears can pinpoint the rustling of a mouse in the darkest wood. Experiments have shown that the long-eared owl and the barn owl can find a dead mouse in light 100 times dimmer than the light needed by the human eye to see anything. And these same owls can locate a live mouse solely by sound in areas that are totally in darkness.

The method of killing used by an owl or a hawk is to plunge at its prey and to strike with hooked claws. As with eyes and bills, each species of bird is fitted with feet designed to help it find and gather up food.

The day-flying birds of prey, ranging from the six-inch-long pygmy falconets of Asia to the great monkey-eating eagle of the Philippines (page 109), feed on almost every animal smaller than themselves. The secretary

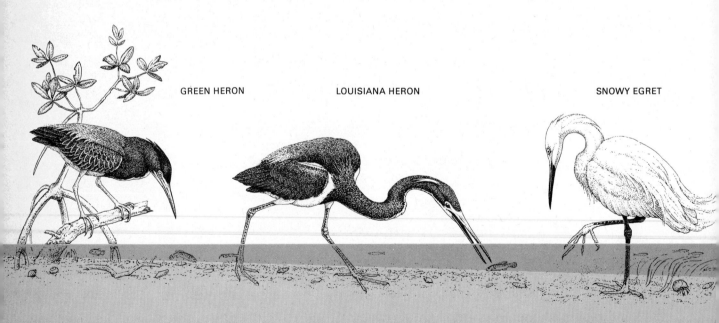

GREEN HERON   LOUISIANA HERON   SNOWY EGRET

bird, so named because it has a score of pen-like quills dangling from behind its ears, specializes in snakes. On its long legs are heavy scales that protect the bird against snake bites.

No bird is better equipped for the pursuit of living prey than the peregrine falcon. It is sleekly streamlined, with a bullet-shaped head, broad shoulders tapering to the tail, and powerful wings. Chasing game, a peregrine goes into a dive estimated to reach 175 miles per hour. But the peregrine is effective only in open country; where dense woodland obstructs its diving flight, the falcon must yield to other birds that are better suited to the landscape.

On the other hand, bird hawks (so called because they eat other birds), are built for

Five Birds of a Feather That Flock and Feed Together

Five varieties of herons, living on the same Florida shoal and eating the same food, survive together by fishing in different ways. The green heron waits in the shallows for fish. The more active Louisiana heron wades out for its food. The snowy egret stirs up the water with its foot to flush out prey. The reddish egret, using its wings as an umbrella, attracts fish to its shadow, then spears them with its bill. Finally, the great blue heron, wading into deeper waters, finds a food supply its shorter-legged cousins cannot reach.

GREAT BLUE HERON

REDDISH EGRET

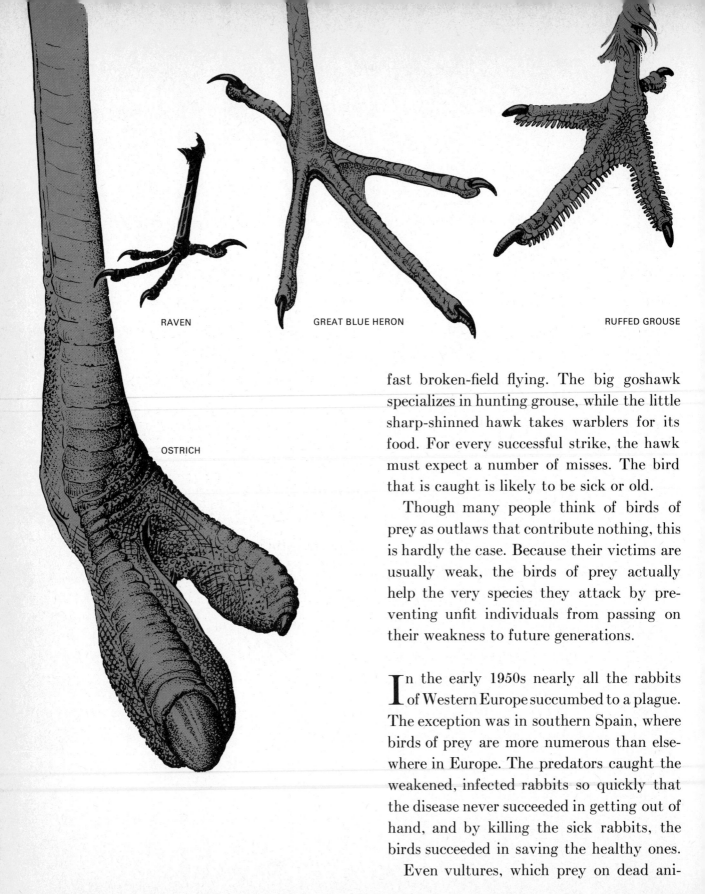

RAVEN

GREAT BLUE HERON

RUFFED GROUSE

OSTRICH

fast broken-field flying. The big goshawk specializes in hunting grouse, while the little sharp-shinned hawk takes warblers for its food. For every successful strike, the hawk must expect a number of misses. The bird that is caught is likely to be sick or old.

Though many people think of birds of prey as outlaws that contribute nothing, this is hardly the case. Because their victims are usually weak, the birds of prey actually help the very species they attack by preventing unfit individuals from passing on their weakness to future generations.

In the early 1950s nearly all the rabbits of Western Europe succumbed to a plague. The exception was in southern Spain, where birds of prey are more numerous than elsewhere in Europe. The predators caught the weakened, infected rabbits so quickly that the disease never succeeded in getting out of hand, and by killing the sick rabbits, the birds succeeded in saving the healthy ones.

Even vultures, which prey on dead ani-

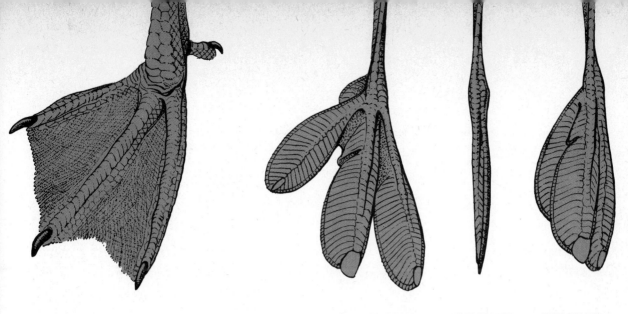

MALLARD DUCK   HORNED GREBE: TOES OPEN   TOES FOLDED (FRONT VIEW)   TOES FOLDED (SIDE VIEW)

mals, perform a vital function in nature's grand design. By eating rotted flesh, vultures prevent the spread of illness, for their digestive system destroys disease-carrying bacteria.

Many species have developed anatomical features to help them in food gathering or eating. The honey buzzard, fond of eating wasps, wears protective armor in the form of hard feathers between the eyes and bill and on the forehead, which makes the sting of the wasp ineffective.

Another strange mechanism belongs to the everglade kite, which feeds only on *Pomacea* snails. This bird carries a deep hook on its bill. For many years ornithologists thought this hook was used to pry snails from their spiral shells, but it is not. Instead the bird patiently holds the snail in its claws until, reassured by the lack of motion, the little creature ventures from its shell; then with a precise jab the bird pierces the snail's nerve center with the hook, paralyzing it.

Every now and then a bird seems to have

Special Shapes of Feet Showing Separate Styles of Life

The shape of a bird's foot reflects its way of life. Like many grazing mammals, the ostrich, which walks in search of food, has a two-toed foot. The raven has an all-purpose foot for perching, walking and scratching. Long toes and small webs keep the marsh-wading heron from sinking in the mud, while the fringes that appear on the grouse's feet every winter help hold it up in snow. The mallard's webbed foot, like the grebe's paddle, is used for swimming. The grebe's toes spread to push against the water; on the return stroke, they fold backward to cut down water resistance.

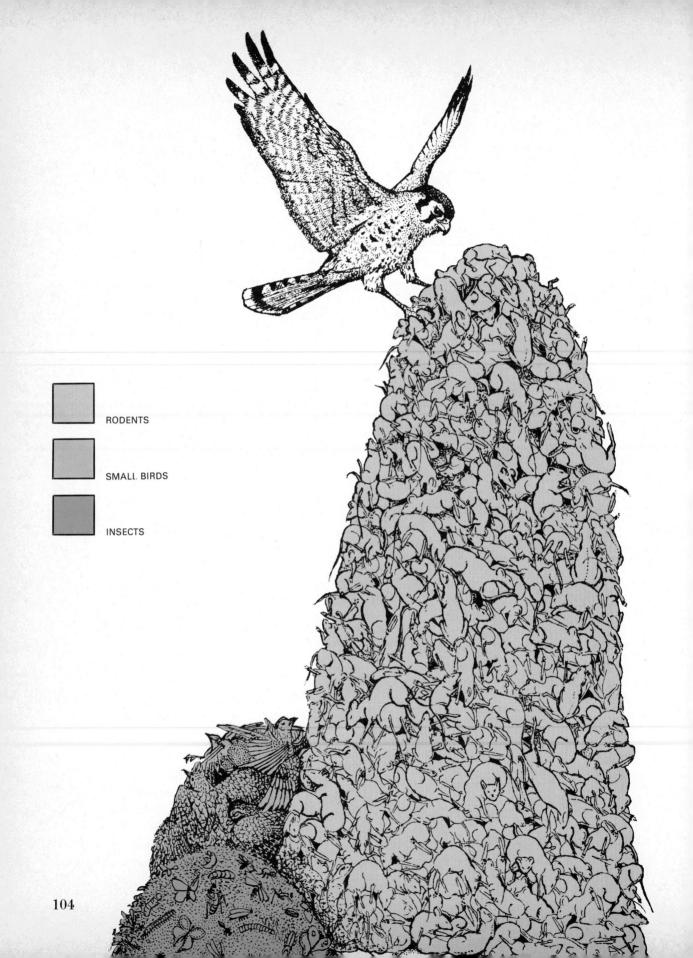

RODENTS

SMALL BIRDS

INSECTS

104

The Predator's Clasping Claw for Picking Up Living Prey

Birds of prey have feet adapted to their habit of feeding on other animals. The claw of an osprey (*right*), a typical predator, tightens by reflex when grasping prey. At left, another predator, the sparrow hawk, is shown with a large pile representing a year's food supply. The smallest pile, 5 per cent of its annual diet, consists of insects; the next, 15 per cent of small birds; the largest, 80 per cent, of rodents. The sparrow hawk may eat nearly 300 mice in a single year.

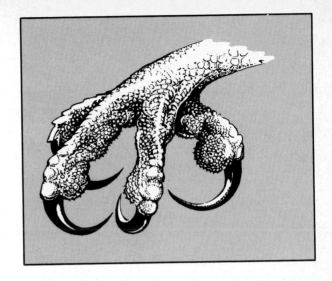

a really odd taste for food. Millions of years ago a vulture, somewhere in Africa, must have idly pecked at the fruit of an oil palm and, finding it edible, made a habit of feeding on the plant. Today the palm-nut vulture eats little else.

In northern South America another extraordinary bird specializes in the oily fruit of palms. This is the oilbird, or guacharo. Related to the whippoorwills and nightjars, the oilbird is the only vegetarian member of an insect-eating order. Seeking ripe fruit at night, it may travel as much as 50 miles from the pitch-dark caves in which it nests. When inside the cave the oilbird finds its way about, not with its eyes but with its voice and ears. Like a bat it emits high-pitched squeaks and then judges its distance from surrounding objects by listening for the echoes as the sound bounces back; the louder the echo the closer the object.

Another specialist, the honey guide, lives on beeswax. This dull-colored bird deliberately attracts the attention of a honey badger, a baboon or even an African tribesman by chattering. Making sure it is being followed, the bird guides its companion to a bees' nest. It waits patiently while its partner steals the honey, then finally helps itself to the bits of honeycomb lying about. For all other creatures, beeswax is inedible, but the honey guide has special bacteria in its intestines that transform the wax into useful food.

Some birds are pirates. The bald eagle often steals an osprey's catch as the smaller bird returns to its nest with a fish. The eagle, bigger, faster and more powerful, frightens the osprey into dropping its catch. Then quickly diving, the eagle snatches the fish before it hits the water.

Frigate birds steal from the boobies. One whole family of birds, the jaegers and skuas —gull-like sea birds—raid gulls and terns to steal their catch.

The widgeon, a dabbling duck, cannot

dive as well as the canvasback. To overcome this handicap the widgeon waits until the canvasback surfaces with a mouthful of wild celery, then rushes in to snatch it away. Laughing gulls use a similar tactic when the brown pelican surfaces with a pouchful of small fish; during the brief moment when the pelican opens its pouch to drain out the water, the gulls dart in to steal a share of the catch.

The Owl and the Magpie: Predators Large and Small

In a sense, the black-billed magpie (*below*) is a bird of prey just as is the great horned owl seen finishing off a snake at left. Though the magpie's victim is only a worm, like any other bird that feeds on other creatures, it could be called a predator. Generally, however, this name is reserved for birds that take on larger animals, from mice and rabbits to small deer. Among these powerful predators are the eagles, which hunt by day, and the owls, which hunt by night.

In contrast to the specialists, some birds eat almost anything. Crows and jays, hungering for a meal, take whatever is close by —young birds, baby mice, insects, grain, fruit or dead animals. But even they prefer some foods to others, and their diets may change with the seasons.

The question is, what is a balanced diet for a bird? Most birds are obviously not too choosy about what they eat. Availability is the key factor. Though a goshawk may prefer grouse for dinner, it will also feed on a pheasant when grouse are scarce. An American robin's appetite for insect eggs does not prevent it from feeding on a tomato worm.

It is unlikely that any bird has ever out-eaten its food supply, for to do so would be to invite eventual starvation. Usually when one item of food becomes scarce the bird turns to something else, while the choice item renews itself. Just as a farmer will sometimes not sell his entire grain crop so that he will have seed to plant the next year, birds seldom eat too deeply into their food, but content themselves with the surplus. In this way a new surplus is assured as the food supply—whether it be animal or vegetable—reproduces and multiplies.

The Airborne Terror of the Tropical Rain Forest

Called the "leopard of the air," an African crowned eagle lives up to its nickname in an attack on a monkey in the rain forest. This bird relies on surprise in its hunting. It makes no noise when it flies, and can turn quickly, using its rounded wings and flexible tail. If the monkey is small, the eagle eats it then and there, letting the bones fall one by one to the ground; its larger victims are probably eaten on the ground.

7

Man: The Bird's Best Friend, Worst Enemy

Although other birds have had a close relationship with man, no bird is so dependent on—and important to—man as the chicken. The many varieties of this bird all share a common ancestor in the species of pheasant called *Gallus gallus*. No one knows exactly when *Gallus gallus* was first domesticated and put on man's dinner table. But recent evidence suggests that Polynesian voyagers, who first carried the fowl to the Hawaiian Islands, also may have introduced a domesticated form of the bird to the New World. Certainly man and the chicken have lived together for at least 5,000 years. For the chicken this relationship has meant protection and a guaranteed supply of food; but the bird pays for this security with its eggs and its meat.

While variants of the original *Gallus gallus* may still be found almost unchanged in the rain forests of Hawaii, the domesticated chicken has been so carefully bred that there are now more than 100 different standard breeds. (A breed is a subgroup of a domesticated species. Members of two different species normally cannot mate, but members of different breeds can and do mate.)

WATTLES GLOWING in the sun, turkeys throng a corral where they are fattened by the scientific care that has made poultry raising a multimillion-dollar industry. Every domestic turkey came from one ancestor, the North American wild turkey. The only other species is the wild turkey of Central America.

111

The Graceful Shapes of Birds Preserved in Ancient Art

Man's love of birds has been expressed in the art of almost every civilization. The red-breasted geese at left were painted in an Egyptian tomb on the Nile 4,600 years ago. These birds are rarely seen now in any country outside of Asia. Below, waterfowl flee an attacker in a decoration inlaid in gold and alloy on a 3,500-year-old Mycenaean dagger. On the opposite page, hooded crows taunt their traditional enemies, the owls, in an old illustration of an Arabic fable.

Chickens have been bred with various goals in mind. Efforts to get high egg production have resulted in hens that can lay an egg nearly every day. Chickens have also been bred for succulent breast meat. And finally, they have been bred for show. Some show breeders have developed chickens with stiltlike legs, or with stubby legs or with every feather turned outward from the body. One of the most extraordinary (as well as most useless) products of the breeders' art is the famous long-tailed fowl of Japan, the *Onagadori*, which sometimes has tail feathers more than 20 feet long.

But the main purpose of chicken breeding remains the production of eggs and meat. Modern technology has played a large part in the vast growth of poultry and egg farming. In the late 19th Century the 500-hen farm was considered a wonder; today poultry operations boast 100,000 hens; some of these are really agricultural factories, in which the chickens spend their lives sitting in cribs stacked several shelves high, while

machines deposit feed beneath their bills.

In the United States poultry raising is now a multibillion-dollar industry. The nation's laying flock numbers about 300 million hens, and nearly two billion more chickens find their way to dining-room tables every year. Egg production is in the neighborhood of 64 billion a year—nearly one egg a day for every man, woman and child in the country.

Duck, goose and turkey raising also contribute significantly to the earnings of the poultry industry. The turkey, one of America's gifts to the world, was unknown in Europe until 16th Century explorers sent some home. Today they are raised in both England and Italy. In the United States more than 100 million turkeys are grown each year, a domesticated population that is very much larger than the number of wild turkeys that lived in the American forests before the Europeans arrived.

Pigeons, too, have been important to man throughout history. According to Biblical legend, Noah was the first human being to take an interest in these birds. The Egyptians raised pigeons for food as early as 3000 B.C., long before chickens were known in that part of the world. Just when pigeons were first used to carry messages is not known, but Julius Caesar employed them 2,000 years ago to send home news of his victories, and these remarkable homing birds continued to play an important role as message bearers right down to the eve of World War II, when radio finally took the major role in military communications.

Today pigeons are still raised by the millions throughout the world—as squabs for eating, as ornamental show birds (*pages 116 and 117*) and as racing birds for competition.

The original "parent" of most, if not all, varieties of domesticated pigeons is the rock dove, which still breeds wild on European sea cliffs. It is likely that wild pigeons first took to town life around the temples of south-

Taking Prey on the Wing: A Noble Bird for a Noble Sport

Hunting with falcons (*below and opposite*) started in Asia, and the sport was fostered in Europe during the Middle Ages by Crusaders. Its popularity with nobles did not die down until nobility itself began to fade. The sport is still practiced in a limited way in parts of Europe and America. Unlike other creatures man has raised for his own purposes, the falcon has never been domesticated; it refuses to breed in captivity.

ROCK DOVE

FANTAIL

Pigeons Made to Order to Suit Man's Inventive Fancies

Man made these pigeons from the pattern of his own imagination. Carefully selecting birds born with odd features, pigeon fanciers produced 300 new varieties from one ancestor, the rock dove (*left, above*). The fantail has become one of the most popular. Traders returning from India probably brought the first pouters to Europe. The feathered hood of the jacobin looks somewhat like the costume of a Jacobin monk.

ern Asia, structures that offered ledges for nests. Today most large cities have their flocks of pigeons, for they offer high stone and brick buildings similar to the ancestral sea cliffs.

Pet birds have probably been part of the homes of men since the Bronze Age, more than 500 centuries ago. But the cheerful canary, the very symbol of all cage birds, did not appear in European homes until the 16th Century when seamen brought it home from the Canary Islands. It proved to be an excellent species for breeders who were able to develop a variety of forms including some very accomplished singers.

It was not until after World War II that supremacy of the canary in the home was challenged by another cage bird, the small parakeet. The millions of these birds in cap-

POUTER

JACOBIN

tivity now probably exceed in numbers the wild parakeets that still throng the water holes of Australia's dry hinterland. In captivity they range in color from clear yellow to blue, but the wild ones are always green.

In North America and in many countries of Europe, laws prevent the caging of most wild birds. In spite of this restriction, the numbers of cage-bird fanciers have multiplied. So great has been the demand for some of the more attractive birds of faraway places that Kenya and other tropical countries have tightened their export restrictions. The ornithologists and the army of amateur bird watchers, who prefer their birds wild and free, do not always see eye to eye with the cage-bird fanciers.

Meanwhile, man also derives considerable profit from the birds he leaves wild. The most useful of these is certainly the guanay cormorant of coastal Peru. The value of its nitrogen-rich droppings on its offshore-island nesting grounds amounts to millions of dollars every year. The Incas of ancient Peru used these droppings as fertilizer for centuries, but it was not until 125 years ago that the deposits of guano, as it is called, became an item of international commerce. During one 25-year period in the 19th Century, Peru shipped out 20 million tons of guano, worth two billion dollars. This so depleted the reserve supplies that the government of Peru restricted sales in order that new reserves could be built up.

This points up the problem of man's greed in his relations with birds. Many species, such as the whooping crane, the Eskimo curlew and several other varieties of water-loving birds, have either disappeared or are

117

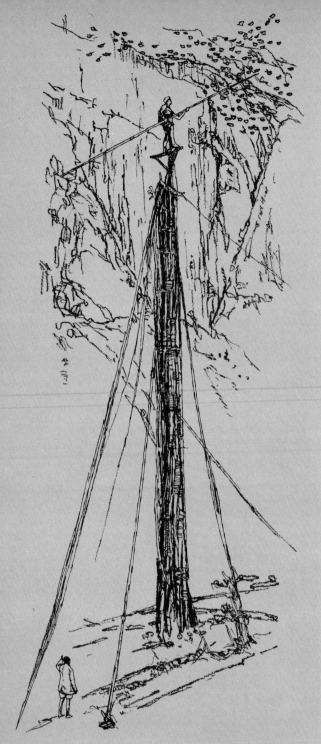

Harvesting Bird's-Nest Soup

Harvesting birds' nests, a collector atop a rickety scaffold scrapes the ceiling of a cavern in North Borneo. These nests are the main ingredient of an unusual Oriental food, bird's-nest soup. Harvesting does little harm to the birds—cave swiftlets—who soon build other nests and lay more eggs.

in danger of vanishing because men have so relentlessly hunted them down for sport, for meat or for feathers. We can do no more than guess at the original duck population of North America. Estimates run between 250 and 500 million. When pioneer trapper Jim Bridger paddled his canoe down the Bear River to Great Salt Lake in Utah, in 1824, ducks darkened the sky in numbers this continent will never see again. Bridger was soon followed by commercial hunters who slaughtered the ducks at will. In 1887 one gunner shot 1,880 birds in a season; another bagged 335 in one day.

The decline in the number of wild ducks was not due only to hunters. The continued draining of swamps and marshes—the natural feeding grounds of ducks—has condemned millions of these birds to starvation. In fact man's indirect attacks on bird life continue to be even more destructive than the gun ever was.

For, as men cut timberland, turn marshes into farms or housing tracts, spray croplands with pesticides and take too many fish from large offshore areas they destroy the shelter and many of the food sources on which numerous birds depend.

As human populations rocket above the three-billion mark, the effect of men on birds—and of birds on men—is certain to increase. Sometimes the birds are viewed (by some men, at least) as villains. In the United States the federal government is faced with continuing demands for measures to

The Last of the Giant Moas
and the Man Who Hunted It

An early native of New Zealand, wearing a whale-tooth pendant and a necklace made from moa thigh-bones, stands half the height of the 12-foot giant he pursued. Between man and moa there was none of the peace that joined falcons and masters or pigeons and breeders. Hunters like this, for whom moa bones and eggs were prized trophies, tracked down these birds and exterminated them by the end of the 13th Century.

Two North American Birds on the Brink of Extinction

The ivory-billed woodpecker (*right*) and the California condor (*left*) are two of North America's rarest birds. The woodpeckers need virgin timber to live in, and few such forests remain. Though none of these birds have been officially spotted in recent years, rumors persist that a few still exist. The condor lived on dead wildlife, then on dead range animals—until settlers switched from ranching to fruit growing. The surviving 58 birds live under government protection.

CALIFORNIA
CONDOR

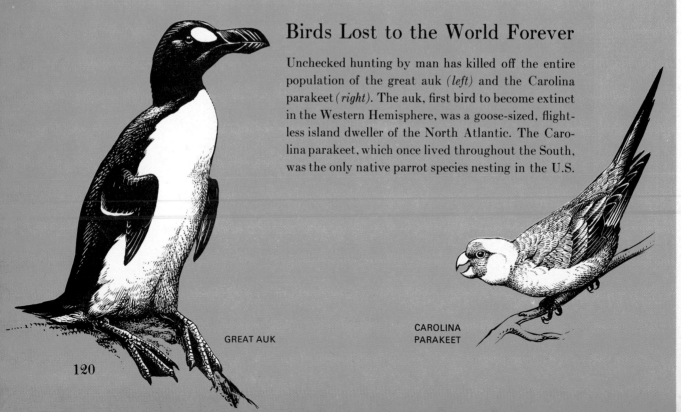

Birds Lost to the World Forever

Unchecked hunting by man has killed off the entire population of the great auk (*left*) and the Carolina parakeet (*right*). The auk, first bird to become extinct in the Western Hemisphere, was a goose-sized, flightless island dweller of the North Atlantic. The Carolina parakeet, which once lived throughout the South, was the only native parrot species nesting in the U.S.

GREAT AUK

CAROLINA
PARAKEET

120

control grackles, red-winged blackbirds and other blackbirds. These species are having a population explosion, largely because they have thrived and multiplied by feeding on the vast wheat and cornfields that American farmers sow. There is, however, a growing number of people who will not hear of such violent methods of population control as poisoning, dynamiting or shooting. These people contend that such methods would be wholesale slaughter, and instead they urge that other means be found to protect farmers' crops from the birds.

What then is the future of birds? Taking the long view, it seems that many birds may eventually disappear because of their inabil-

IVORY-BILLED
WOODPECKER

121

ity to adapt to a rapidly changing world. Sixty or 70 million years ago, cranes, rails, bustards and their relatives, for example, made up a far larger portion of the world's bird population than they do today.

Since late in the 17th Century nearly 80 species have become extinct. The years of greatest loss were at the turn of this century; some 20 species disappeared between 1885 and 1905 alone. The heaviest mortality was among birds native to islands. Continental birds can often survive man-made disaster by flying to uninhabited areas; but island birds, with their backs to the sea, have no place to retreat. Some island dwellers like the dodo, shown opposite, and the great auk, being unable to fly away, were ruthlessly slaughtered; others vanished because man introduced rats, goats, cats, rabbits and mongooses to their island homes; these four-legged animals prey on birds or consume their food supply. Still others disappeared when their island nesting grounds were converted into farms.

Today, at least 100 species are threatened with extinction and may soon disappear, even though man has now taken steps to protect them through wildlife preserves and bans on hunting. Yet sometimes, just when we think there is no hope for a species, it manages to adapt to change and revive. The pileated woodpecker, just like its cousin the ivory-billed woodpecker, was once thought to be on the road to extinction. But unlike the ivory-bill, the pileated woodpecker was able to adapt to the cutover forests, and today the bird is flourishing once again.

If man has caused some birds to disappear, he is also responsible for the prosperity of others. Robins, song sparrows, chipping sparrows, yellow warblers, swifts and swallows are only a few of the many species that have benefited from man-made surroundings—farms, towns, gardens, orchards. Barn and cliff swallows, for example, find barns and bridges better nesting sites than the cliffs and caves they formerly used.

In particular, the perching birds—more than three fifths of today's bird population—continue to prosper. Among these birds, the many seed eaters—weaverbirds, sparrows, finches and their allies—are the most numerous and perhaps the most adaptable to changing conditions. Of all birds these may have the most promising future. Nectar feeders, and insect eaters, too, may well survive man-made changes in their surroundings. Increased cultivation of the soil and planting of crops would even seem to assure the prosperity of some species—unless they are killed off by chemical sprays that poison the insects, seeds and berries that make up their diet.

It is quite certain that as our cities mature their shade trees and gardens will harbor more birds than ever. In England's old

Dodos: Easy Prey for Four-footed Predators

The dodo (*foreground*) of the Indian Ocean island of Mauritius is a symbol of extinction. Because it could not fly, it was an easy prey for pigs and rats brought in by settlers. By 1681, it had vanished. The white dodo in the background, from Reunion Island, was wiped out 65 years later.

suburban gardens and estates, there are as many as 30 birds per acre, or far more than in the most hospitable natural woods.

Since the beginning of the century, when the destruction of certain birds for their colorful feathers became a public scandal, American and Canadian progress in bird protection has set an example to the rest of the world. In other areas, the record is less commendable. Some Latin American countries offer almost no protection. While northwestern Europe cherishes birds, some Mediterranean countries still shoot or cage birds with no thought of the future. Elsewhere, in the U.S.S.R., India and Japan, people recognize the need for bird protection.

Yet even in the United States the record is spotty. Many birds are safe from hunters, but may not be protected from commercial or industrial developers who destroy natural surroundings A man cannot pick up a gun and shoot an oriole in his backyard, but he can chop down a tree that holds an oriole's nest and family. Duck hunting without a license is forbidden, but very little thought is given to ducks when a swamp where they feed is drained.

Worst of all are the pesticides farmers use to protect their crops. These chemical sprays kill birds both directly, by poisoning them, and indirectly, by destroying the insects on which some birds feed.

Recently in the Midwest, an effort was made to save elm trees from disease by spraying them with DDT. The result was at least half a million dead robins, killed when the chemical found its way into their bodies.

Today the public is aware of the dangerous effects of chemical sprays, and research is underway to find less harmful poisons than those now being used, for in time, present-day pesticides could destroy all our bird life. Certainly a world without birds or a spring without song would be incomplete for any man; for some such an unhappy prospect would be quite intolerable.

Millions of Bird Watchers: The Birds' Dedicated Friends

Dedicated bird watchers, like these making a bird census at dawn in Washington, D.C., work for the preservation of bird life. In North America, where four species have died out since Europeans arrived, some five to 11 million bird watchers attend to the safety of the 650 species that still breed there. The author of this book is standing second from the left.

Index

Numerals in italics indicate a photograph or painting of the subject listed.

For Further Reading

Allen, Robert Porter, *The Giant Golden Book of Birds.* Golden Press, 1962.

Austing, G. Ronald, and John B. Holt, Jr., *The World of the Great Horned Owl.* Lippincott, 1966.

Austing, G. Ronald, *The World of the Red-tailed Hawk.* Lippincott, 1964.

Brodtkorb, Reidar, *Flying Free.* Rand McNally, 1964.

Cosgrove, Margaret, *Eggs— And What Happens Inside Them.* Dodd, Mead, 1966.

Cruickshank, Allan and Helen, *1,001 Questions Answered About Birds.* Dodd, Mead, 1958.

Darling, Louis, *The Gull's Way.* William Morrow, 1965.

Earle, Olive L., *Birds and Their Beaks.* William Morrow, 1965.

Froman, Robert, *Our Fellow Immigrants.* David McKay, 1965.

Gilbert, Bil, *How Animals Communicate.* Pantheon Books, 1966.

Hylander, Clarence J., *Feathers and Flight.* Macmillan, 1959.

Kieran, John, *An Introduction to Birds.* Doubleday, 1965.

Lewellen, John Bryan, *Birds and Planes: How They Fly.* Crowell, 1953.

McCoy, J. J., *The Hunt for the Whooping Cranes.* Lothrop, Lee & Shepard, 1966.

Peterson, Roger Tory: *A Field Guide to the Birds.*

Houghton Mifflin, 1947. *A Field Guide to Western Birds.* Houghton Mifflin, 1961.

Ripper, Charles L., *Diving Birds.* William Morrow, 1967.

Selsam, Millicent E.: *Animals as Parents.* William Morrow, 1965. *The Courtship of Animals.* William Morrow, 1964. *How Animals Live Together.* William Morrow, 1963. *How Animals Tell Time.* William Morrow, 1967. *The Language of Animals.* William Morrow, 1962.

Smith, Dick, and Robert Easton, *California Condor, Vanishing American.* McNally and Loftin, 1964.

Stever, H. Guyford, James J.

Haggerty, and the Editors of LIFE, *Flight.* Time Inc., 1965.

Storer, John H., *The Flight of Birds.* Cranbrook Institute of Science, 1948.

Sutton, Ann and Myron, *Animals on the Move.* Rand McNally, 1965.

Vessel, Matthew F., and Herbert H. Wong, *Introducing Our Western Birds.* Fearon Publishers, Inc., 1965.

Wakefield, John, *The Strange World of Birds.* Macrae Smith, 1963.

Wong, Herbert H., *Ducks, Geese, and Swans.* Lane Book Company, 1960.

Wright, Dare, *Look at a Gull.* Random House, 1967.

Credits

The sources for the illustrations that appear in this book are shown below. Credits for the pictures from left to right are separated by commas, from top to bottom by dashes.

Cover—By Jerry Cooke from Photo Researchers Inc.

Table of contents—Rudolf Freund—Lois and Louis Darling—Roger Tory Peterson—Guy Tudor—Peter Parnell—Lois and Louis Darling—Bob Kuhn

6, 7—Rudolf Freund

9—Roger Tory Peterson, Virginia Wells

10, 11—Roger Tory Peterson

12—John Dominis

14, 15—Roger Tory Peterson

16—Guy Tudor, Virginia Wells

18, 19—Dmitri Kessel

20, 21—Guy Tudor

22—N. R. Farbman

23—Guy Tudor

25—William Vandivert

26—Andreas Feininger

28 to 31—Lois and Louis Darling

33—Rudolf Freund

34, 35—Rudolf Freund based on pen and camera studies in *Prairie Wings* by Edgar M. Queeny and Richard E. Bishop

36, 37—Rudolf Freund based on drawings in *Hummingbirds* by Dale Astle

38, 39—Andreas Feininger

40, 41, 42—Leonard McCombe

43—William J. Johoda from National Audubon Society—J. R. Eyerman

44, 45—Jean Held

46 to 49—Maps by Adolph E. Brotman, birds by Roger Tory Peterson

51—Gordon Coster

52—David Goodnow

54, 55—Lois and Louis Darling

57, 58, 59—Guy Tudor

60, 61—Lois and Louis Darling

62, 63—Landscapes by Ara Derderian, birds by Roger Tory Peterson

64—Lee Boltin

66—Thomas D. McAvoy

68—Guy Tudor

69, 70—Peter Parnell

71, 72—Guy Tudor

73—Roger Tory Peterson

74, 75—Guy Coheleach

76, 77—Jack J. Kunz

79—Roger Tory Peterson

81—Official Navy Photo by Walter M. Cox

82, 83—Robert W. Mitchell

84, 85—Joe Scherschel

87—Dmitri Kessel

88, 89—Shelly Grossman

90—Lois and Louis Darling

91—Canadian Wild-life Service—Guy Tudor

92, 93—Adolph E. Brotman

94, 95—Lois and Louis Darling

98, 99—Lois and Louis Darling

except extreme left centre René Martin

100, 101—Guy Tudor

102, 103—Lois and Louis Darling

104—Peter Parnell

105—Lois and Louis Darling

106, 107—Shelly Grossman

108, 109—Guy Tudor

110—Alfred Eisenstaedt

112, 113—James Whitmore courtesy Department of Antiquities, Government of Egypt—Larry Burrows courtesy National Museum Athens, courtesy Bibliothèque Nationale, Paris

114, 115—Jack J. Kunz

116, 117—Bob Kuhn

118—Anthony Saris

119—Guy Tudor

120, 121—Roger Tory Peterson

123—Guy Tudor

125—Francis Miller

Acknowledgments

The editors are indebted to the staff of the LIFE Nature Library, from which this volume is adapted; the staff for this edition: Stanley Fillmore, editor; Eric Gluckman, designer; Peter Chaitin and Victor Waldrop, writers; Eleanor Feltser, Susan Marcus and Theo Pascal, researchers; Eleanore W. Karsten, copyreader, Virginia Wells, art assistant.